SPSS FROM A to Z

A Brief Step-by-Step Manual

for

Psychology, Sociology and Criminal Justice

Richard C. Sprinthall
American International College

PEARSON

Boston   New York   San Francisco
Mexico City   Montreal   Toronto   London   Madrid   Munich   Paris
Hong Kong   Singapore   Tokyo   Cape Town   Sydney

ISBN-13: 978-0-205-62698-4
ISBN-10:   0-205-62698-X

Printed in the United States of America

10 9 8 7 6 5 4 3   12 11 10 09

BEFORE YOU BEGIN

This manual provides 26 problems (labeled A to Z) to solve via the SPSS program. All will be fully explained, and many can be done even by a first-time user. The problems range from the most basic, such as measures of central tendency, to more sophisticated techniques, such as factor analysis. Before beginning the problems, however, please read the introductory section in order to get acquainted with the SPSS format. This introduction contains such procedures as defining the variables, entering data, changing the column width, inserting new rows or columns, deleting rows or columns, moving and copying data, and SAVING your files.

PROBLEMS: A to Z

The problems to be done on SPSS are as follows:

IMPORTANT NOTE: Sometimes SPSS reports a probability of alpha error at .000. In point of fact alpha can NEVER actually be zero, but when rounded out several places the resulting value sometimes rounds to zero.

To the Student

As you go through this manual, please keep uppermost in mind that SPSS is only a tool, a very powerful tool to be sure, but still a tool. It's like a skill-saw to a carpenter. The skill-saw doesn't build the house - the carpenter does. The tool can't do the work without guidance from someone with a knowledge base of statistical rules and research procedures. You will come to realize that SPSS is easy to learn, perhaps even too easy, but SPSS alone is not going to do the whole job. You still need a textbook (see Sprinthall, 2007) and a class instructor to fill you in on the theoretical backgrounds and the legitimate uses of all these statistical techniques that the program puts at your fingertips. You are really blessed that you have the SPSS windows version, versus the "good old days" of complicated, unforgiving syntax.

Inputting Data

These problems will be done on very small samples, far smaller than you will read about in the real world of research. However to prevent you from spending an inordinate amount of time typing in data, the sample sizes have been kept deliberately limited (so that you can use your time running and understanding the analyses). In short, if you can do a Pearson r on a sample of 10 subjects, you can do it on 100 subjects. The procedure is the same. However, you must learn how to input data. In this manual we don't provide you with a prepackaged CD full of data from which to do the various analyses. It is absolutely crucial that you become familiar with typing in the data yourself and then SAVING your data files.

INTRODUCTION: PROGRAM INSTRUCTIONS FOR SPSS

Before doing any statistical analyses, you should spend a few minutes just getting used to the SPSS format. SPSS for Windows uses a regular spreadsheet arrangement, just like Lotus, Quattro and Excel. That is, there are columns (which are headed by variable names), and rows (which refer to the cases or the subject numbers). Also, keep in mind that the intersection of a column and a row is called a cell.

The Opening Window Shows the Following:

The Title Bar
On the top row of the window you will see what is called the Title Bar, on which (at the far right) are three choices, ▣ (to minimize the screen), ▣ (to maximize the screen) and ▣ (to quit the screen). It is best to ▣, maximize.

The Menu Bar
The next row down is called the Menu Bar, and it goes from File on the far left to Help on the far right. Most of our analytic work will be chosen from this bar.

The Tool Bar
Just below the Menu is the Tool Bar, which goes from an icon for Open File on the far left to an icon for Use Sets on the far right. As you can see, this tool bar also includes the Print Command icon.

The Task Bar
At the very bottom of the screen is the Task Bar, which shows Data View, Variable View and (once you've completed an analysis) the Output Viewer.

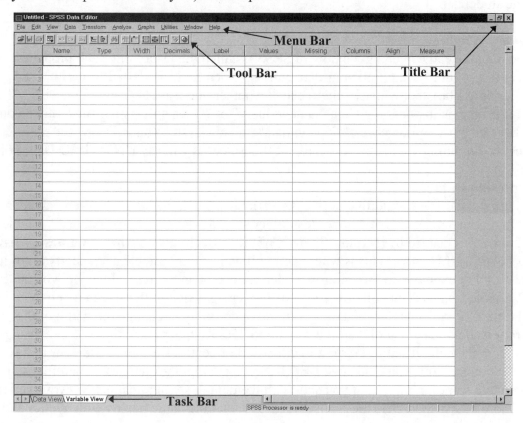

The Three Main Windows

1. The Data Editor Window
This window opens automatically as soon as you start the SPSS program. It will be used to input data, store data on the spreadsheet, and run the various statistical tests.

2. The Variable View Window
This window allows you to name your variables, such as IQ, or whatever it is that you're measuring. It also let's you   set the width of your cells and set the number of decimal places.

3. The Output Window
This third window can only be seen AFTER you have generated some results. This is where the results of your tests are shown, and they can be seen as numbers, tables and/or graphs. It also can be used to print your output. In this manual we will only concentrate on those outputs that are the most crucial for the beginning statistics student. We call it **Selected Output.** You can easily switch between the various windows screens by clicking on the Task Bar at the bottom of the screen.

SELECTED OUTPUT

In the sections to follow, you will be reading about SELECTED OUTPUT. Thus, you will be given only the most basic results for your interpretation. SPSS, remember, is used not only by students new to the field, but also by world-class statisticians interpreting very sophisticated research strategies. So that you won't be drowning in the large number of output pages SPSS provides, we will focus only on those results appropriate to the level of sophistication needed by the average student.

The Opening Window
As pointed out above, the opening window in SPSS is called the Data Editor and produces the spreadsheet that will be used for all your data entries. When SPSS is started, superimposed on the Data Editor is a box that will ask you to check whether you want to "run the tutorial," "Type in data," "Run an existing query," "Create a new query" or "Open an existing file." Since you don't yet have an existing file, check "Type in data" and click OK. You will now see the spreadsheet for inputting your data. At the top of this screen it will say UNTITLED Data Editor.

Before Entering Data
Before entering data, you should first define the variables. Click the Variable View tab near the bottom-left of your screen, and you now see another spreadsheet screen, called the "Variable View" window. It's headed by: **Name Type Width Decimals Label Values Missing Columns Align Measure.** This is where you will name your variable and specify all of its characteristics. For example, in the first row under name type in Scores (which we will use as our first Variable Name). You will now see at the lower right side of the screen a button called Column Format. If you click this, you are given the opportunity to change the width of the column from its default setting of 8 all the way up to 256. Also, it is here that you can change the alignment from the default setting of right to either left or center. Be sure to use your mouse to highlight the column you want to change BEFORE you attempt the changes. When first setting up your variable names, it's best that you stay with the default setting, that is keep your variable names no more than 8 characters long. Also make sure that the name begins with a letter and that

there are no spaces in between the letters. One caution: because SPSS uses certain letter combinations for other procedures, you can't use any of the following as variable names—all, and, by, eg, ge, gt, it, le, ne, not, or, with.

Next, click on the cell in the next column to the right (under Type) and click on the little gray box. A pop-up box will then appear that allows you to specify a variety of choices. Leave the check mark (the default setting) next to numeric. This will be your choice 99% of the time, because you will want the vast majority of your entries to be treated as numbers. The only time you would want to check "string" is when you are using letters only or combining letters and numbers, such as entering a subject's name alone or the name and then perhaps an identification number. For width, the default setting is 8, which will work most of the time. However, when typing a long string, such as a long last name or identification number, you will need to increase the width of the column. For decimal places, the default setting is 2, but your instructor may want you to increase it to 3 or perhaps even more. The next column, Label, allows you to add text to any variable whose name is not immediately obvious. For instance, you have defined your variable as Scores, but with Label you can indicate precisely what the score is, for example it might be a Math score and was obtained on such and such a date. The Label option lets you use up to 256 characters, and its width will change automatically as you keep entering more characters. For the problems that follow you can leave this option blank. When you click the next column, Values, another pop-up screen appears and you can identify your variables by number. For example, suppose you are using 0 for male and 1 for female, this is where you enter the codes, and this is where the program will REMEMBER which was which. The next column, "Missing", is used when a subject has refused to answer one of your questions, perhaps ethnic background or even gender. You may want to code these with a number, such as 1, 2 etc. The next column, "Columns" allows you to set the width of each of your columns. As already mentioned, the default setting is 8, but for some of your variables you may need only 3 or 4 spaces. The fewer spaces you use, the more of your spreadsheet will be visible on a single screen. Finally, under "Measure" you can choose which measurement scale your data are portraying. "Scale" is used to cover both ratio and interval data, and the other two measures, ordinal and nominal, will become obvious as we continue through our lesson. When you finish, click the data view tab at the bottom of the screen and your data editor screen will reappear. Before entering any new data always Click File, New, and Data.

CHECK BOXES AND RADIO BUTTONS

There are two methods of selection in the dialog boxes. With check boxes, use your mouse to click on the box next to any or all the options you want to select. For the radio buttons, those little circles, you can only select one at a time. Once you select one, all the others are automatically turned off, just like the buttons on your car radio - one station at a time. Once you make your radio selection, a little dot appears in the selected circle.

INSERTING NEW ROWS OR COLUMNS

There may be times when you decide to add a new row or column to your spreadsheet. For example, let's say you have a column for age and next to it a column for IQ. You decide to put a column for gender in between these two. Move the cursor to the column, which is directly to the RIGHT of where you want the new column to be. Click Data and then Insert Variable. The new variable is going to automatically be called VAR00001, so go back to the Variable View screen and type in the name of the new variable in the appropriate row. To insert a new row the procedure is virtually the same except that after clicking Data you must check Insert Case. Keep your cursor on the cell just above the place where you want the new row. This could be useful if you notice that you forgot to put in the score for Case # 5, but you have already inadvertently used that row for Case # 6.

DELETING A COLUMN

To delete a column, click on the top of the column you want to get rid of and press the delete key.

DELETING A ROW

To delete a row, click on the far left side of the row, and use the mouse to drag across the row. Press the delete key.

MOVING AND COPYING DATA

MOVE – this is the procedure to use if you want to move a section of the spreadsheet from one place to another. Use the mouse to drag over the area to be moved (it must be a rectangular area), and then click Edit and Cut. Move the cursor to the cell in the UPPER LEFT HAND CORNER of where you want the data to go. Click Edit, and click Paste.

COPY – If you want to copy a section of the spreadsheet to another location, so that you will have it in both locations, then you must again begin by dragging over the area you want to copy. Then click Edit and Copy. Move the cursor to the upper left-hand corner of where you want to put the data and click Edit and Paste.

OK, you're now ready. Let's get started!

PROBLEM A

Entering and retrieving data.
Click the **Variable View** tab at the bottom of your screen and type scores in the first row. Now click back to the **Data View** screen and you will find the column labeled and available for data entry. Now put the cursor under the first column, which you previously set up as Scores, and enter the data shown below.

Case	Scores
1.	10
2.	8
3.	6
4.	4
5.	2

Once the data are entered, check to see if you have any data entry errors. If you find an error, put the cursor over that score, and type in the correct value and enter it.

SAVING THE FILE

Much wasted time and many long lamentations have resulted from forgetting to file save. Don't let it happen to you. Remember, if the electricity goes off, the lights will come back on, but your data will be GONE. Once the data are in, Click on file in the top left corner of the screen and then click Save as. The screen then allows you to select where you want to save the file. Click the pull-down menu beside the word Desktop. Your screen will offer you the following choices: Desktop, My Documents, My Computer, 3.5 Floppy (A), (C), (D), (E), and Network Neighborhood. If you have an A drive and a disk in your A drive you can save it to your floppy by clicking the 3.5 drive A. Or you can opt for My Documents and save it on your C drive, or use D or E and save it on a flash drive. Regardless of where you put it, just make sure to SAVE IT. Then on a line a few spaces below, next to your file name, type in the file name you've created. Let's call it PROBA, for problem A. Now click save, and you are ready to roll.

RETRIEVING THE FILE

For practice, click file and then exit. Now load the SPSS program again, click **Open an Existing Data Source** and **OK**. Now click the place where you left the file, for example in My Documents. You will then find your file name, **PROBA**.

Click on the file name and **Open**. The data will quickly appear, and your screen will look like this:

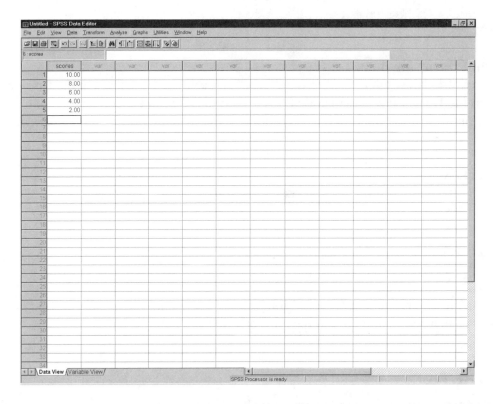

Before getting too far ahead, it might be interesting see a little of what SPSS can do for you.

Step by Step

1. Click **Analyze**,
2. Then click **Descriptive Statistics**. And when that screen appears, click **Descriptives**.

Your screen will look like this:

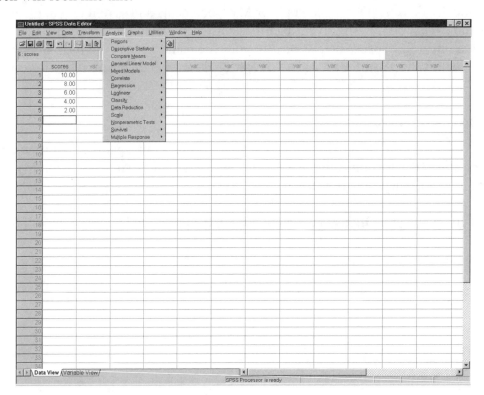

3. Next, click on **scores** and then click the small arrowhead key in the middle of the screen.

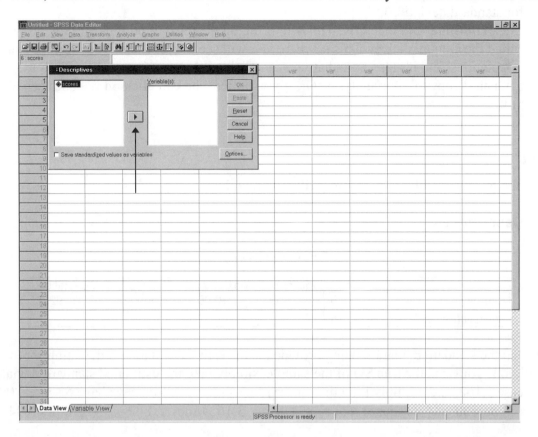

This will move the scores into the box on the right. Your screen will look like this:

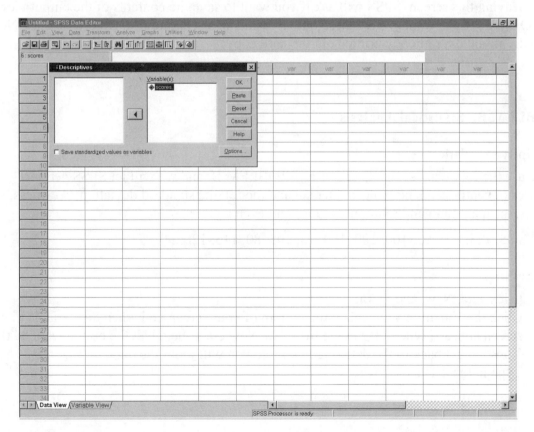

4. Now click on **Options** and check the **Mean** and the **Std deviation** (which is SPSS speak for standard deviation).
5. Click **continue**, and then **OK**. This will bring up the third important SPSS window, called the Output Viewer. This is where you will see the results of your various statistical calculations, and it's also here that you can click on the print icon on the SPSS toolbar to get a hard copy of your analyses. Or, if you prefer, you can click on file and then click print.

OUTPUT

For the above data, the output navigator will look like this:

Descriptives

Descriptive Statistics

	N	Minimum	Maximum	Mean	Std. Deviation
scores	5	2.00	10.00	6.0000	3.16228
Valid N (listwise)	5				

Notice that the standard deviation being provided is the estimated standard deviation for the population. If you need the true SD of the sample, simply take the estimated standard deviation (in this case 3.162, and multiply it by the square root of (N-1/N). Since we have 5 scores, (N-1/N) = 4/5, or .800, and its square root = .894. Thus, 3.162 times $\sqrt{.800}$ = 3.162 times .894 = 2.826.

Before leaving this screen, SPSS will ask if you want to save the contents of the output viewer. Click OK only if you want to save these output results in a separate file. Otherwise click NO, especially if you have already printed out the hard copy.

PROBLEM B: Statistical Analysis

Descriptive Statistics
Please use the following set of IQ scores as PROBLEM B, and we will let SPSS get our measures of central tendency (mean, median and mode), the standard deviation, skewness, kurtosis, the maximum and minimum values and even a graph.

110, 75, 85, 125, 105, 95, 100, 100, 100, 95, 105, 80, 115, 120, 90

Step-by-Step
1. Click **File**, **New**, and **Data**.
2. Click the **Variable View** tab at the bottom of your screen and when the variable view screen appears, type in **IQ** in the first row. Now click the tab at the bottom called "**Data View**" to get back to the data screen (where you will input the data).
3. Type in the data as follows:

Case	iq
1.	110
2.	75
3.	85
4.	125
5.	105
6.	95
7.	100
8.	100
9.	100
10.	95
11.	105
12.	80
13.	115
14.	120
15.	90

Now before going any further click **file**. Then SAVE the data by clicking on **Save as** and then click on the arrow to the right of the pull-down menu that says desktop. Select your save location. Then toward the bottom, next to the line that says file name, type in the file name we will now create. Let's call it **PROBB**, (for Problem B) so you will know which data set it contains. You are now ready to click **Save**, and at that point your data become safely stored.

4. Click **Analyze**, then **Descriptive Statistics**.
5. Click **Descriptives**, and then **Frequencies**.
6. Move **IQ** into the **Variables** box by clicking on the little arrowhead in the middle of the screen and then check **Statistics**.
7. Now check **Mean, Median, Mode, Range, Std. deviation, Skewness, Kurtosis, Minimum** and **Maximum**.
8. Click **Continue** and then click **Charts** and select Histogram.
9. Click **Continue** and **OK**.

Selected Output:
Your screen will look like this:

Frequencies

iq

N	Valid	15
	Missing	0
Mean		100.0000
Median		100.0000
Mode		100.00
Std. Deviation		14.14214
Skewness		.000
Std. Error of Skewness		.580
Kurtosis		-.404
Std. Error of Kurtosis		1.121
Range		50.00
Minimum		75.00
Maximum		125.00

Histogram

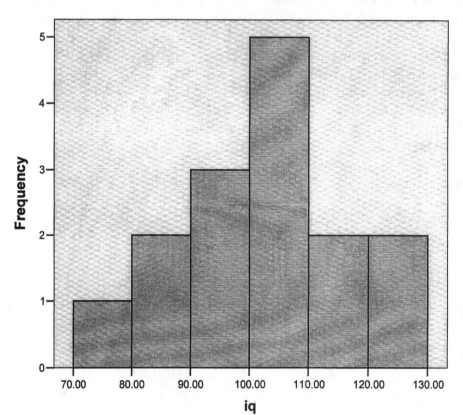

Mean = 100.00
Std. Dev. = 14.14214
N = 15

10

SORTING THE DATA

There are numerous times when it is necessary to sort the data into some kind of meaningful order. Let's say you've spent an hour entering hundreds of IQ scores and you want to put them in order (either high-to-low or low-to-high).

Step by Step

1. Click **Data** and **Sort Cases**. When the Sort Cases box appears, a list of the variables on your spreadsheet is shown.
2. Click on **IQ** (which is the file you just created) and move it, via the arrowhead button over into the **Sort By** box.
3. Now check whether it's ascending or descending. For the IQ scores let's put the highest score at the top, so check **descending**.
4. Click **OK**. You will then have sorted the entire spreadsheet and you will NOT have lost your subject-data linkages.

PROBLEM C

Finding Standard Scores

To find the z scores for each raw score, please use the same data set as shown above. To bring up the data, click on **Retrieve**, then the location and then click on **PROBB**.

Step-by-Step

1. Click **Analyze**, **Descriptive statistics** and **Descriptives**. Put iq in the Variables box. And then check **Save standardized values as variables** (which is in the lower left corner).
2. Click on **Windows** and check **OK**.
3. Then check the **Data Editor** tab to get back to the spreadsheet.

You will now find that right beside each of your IQ scores is a new column called **ziq**. For each raw score the corresponding z score is now shown.

	iq	Ziq
1	110.00	.70711
2	75.00	-1.76777
3	85.00	-1.06066
4	125.00	1.76777
5	105.00	.35355
6	95.00	-.35355
7	100.00	.00000
8	100.00	.00000
9	100.00	.00000
10	95.00	-.35355
11	105.00	.35355
12	80.00	-1.41421
13	115.00	1.06066
14	120.00	1.41421
15	90.00	-.70711

INFERENTIAL STATISTICS

PROBLEM D

Single Sample t test.

For this example, please use the following data:
98, 85, 82, 81, 81, 80, 79, 79, 78, 64.

We will now test the hypothesis that this sample could represent a population whose mean is 80.

Step-by-Step

1. Click **File**, **New**, and **Data**.
2. Click the **Variable View** tab at the bottom of your screen and when the Variable View screen appears type in **Scores** in the first row. Now click the tab at the bottom called **Data View** to get back to the data screen.
3. Enter the data shown below.

Case	scores
1	98
2	85
3	82
4	81
5	81
6	80
7	79
8	79
9	78
10	64

Save the file as **PROBD.**

4. Click **Analyze**. **Compare means**, and **One Sample t**.
5. Put **scores** in as the **Test Variable**.
6. Enter the **Test Value**, which in this case is **80** (the given parameter mean).
7. **OK**.

SELECTED OUTPUT

One-Sample Statistics

	N	Mean	Std. Deviation	Std. Error Mean
scores	10	80.7000	8.24688	2.60789

One-Sample Test

	Test Value = 80					
					95% Confidence Interval of the Difference	
	t	df	Sig. (2-tailed)	Mean Difference	Lower	Upper
scores	.268	9	.794	.70000	-5.1995	6.5995

Conclusion:
A single sample t was computed comparing the sample mean with a known population mean of 80. The difference was not significant. Because no significant difference was found (t (9) = .268, p > .05), the null hypothesis was accepted. Therefore, this sample could be representative of the known population.

PROBLEM E
Two Sample t test.
Two random samples were selected from a population of inmates in a county Correctional Center for the treatment of alcohol addiction. Group 1 was given three months of substance abuse therapy, while the inmates in Group 2 were left to their regular activities at the center (and in this case did not include the treatment). Both groups were then measured on an Alcohol Abuse Test, the AAT. Their AAT scores (with the higher scores indicating a more positive prognosis) were as follows:

Group 1: 14, 15, 10, 9, 14, 10, 14, 15, 11, 8.
Group 2: 10, 7, 7, 8, 7, 4, 7, 5, 3, 2.

Step-by-Step
1. Click **File**, **New**, and **Data**.
2. Click the **Variable View** tab at the bottom of your screen and when the Variable View screen appears type **Group** in the first row and **Scores** in the second row. Tab back to the **Data Editor** and enter the following:

Case	group	scores
1	1	14
2	1	15
3	1	10
4	1	9
5	1	14
6	1	10
7	1	14
8	1	15
9	1	11
10	1	8
11	2	10
12	2	7
13	2	7
14	2	8
15	2	7
16	2	4
17	2	7
18	2	5
19	2	3
20	2	2

Save as **PROBE**
3. Click **Analyze, Compare Means,** and **Independent Samples t Test.**
4. Put **Scores** in the **Test Variable Box**.
5. Put **Group** in as the **Grouping Variable**.
6. Click **Define Groups**.
7. In the **Group 1 box** type **1** and in the **Group 2** box type **2**.
8. Click **Continue** and **OK**

Your screen will look like this:

Independent Samples Test

		t-test for Equality of Means			
		t	df	Sig. (2-tailed)	Mean Difference
scores	Equal variances assumed	5.240	18	.000	6.00000
	Equal variances not assumed	5.240	17.872	.000	6.00000

T-Test

Group Statistics

	group	N	Mean	Std. Deviation	Std. Error Mean
scores	1.00	10	12.0000	2.66667	.84327
	2.00	10	6.0000	2.44949	.77460

Independent Samples Test

		Levene's Test for Eqaulity of Variances	
		F	Sig.
scores	Equal variances assumed Equal variances not assumed	.706	.412

Conclusion:
A two-sample independent t test was computed and found to be equal to 5.240, which is clearly significant (t (18) = 3.106, p < .01). In fact SPSS lists the significance probability as .000, which of course is far below either .05 or .01. As we said before, the significance cannot ever actually be zero, but the SPSS program rounded it to zero. Thus, the researcher concluded that the substance abuse treatment significantly improved performance on the AAT, and pointed to a significantly more positive outcome. In short, the treatment worked.

Please also note that the Levene test results were also provided. The Levene test is a test of the homogeneity of variance, one of the requirements for the t test. This is a basic assumption of the t test, which demands that the variability within each of the two sample groups be similar. The Levene test produces an F ratio, which if NOT SIGNIFICANT assures us that the homogeneity requirement has been met. If the F ratio had been significant (a p value of .05 or less) we would have to interpret on the basis of equal variances NOT ASSUMED. In the output shown below, we find that the Levene F ratio is only .706 and the significance level is .412, far above the .05 level. We are safe in assuming that the homogeneity of variance criterion has been met.

PROBLEM F

Pearson r
A researcher wishes to investigate the possible relationship between psychopathy (as measured by the SS scale on the HPSI (Holden Psychological Screening Inventory) and scores on the LSI (Level of Service Inventory). The LSI is used in prisons to determine how serious a security threat a given resident might be while incarcerated. The LSI is scored for security risk such that scores of 0 to 2 indicate a low risk, 3 to 5 a medium risk and 6 to 8 a high risk. A group of 10 incarcerated felons was randomly selected from the population at a certain state prison and given the two tests during orientation. Their scores follow:

Case	SS	LSI
1	8	3
2	7	2
3	15	5
4	17	6
5	27	8
6	12	6
7	8	3
8	22	7
9	13	5
10	11	4

For this procedure the scores must be listed side by side.

Step-by-Step
1. Click **File**, **New**, and **Data**.
2. Click the **Variable View** tab at the bottom of your screen and when the Variable View screen appears type **SS** in the first row and **LSI** in the second row. Now click the **Data View** tab at the bottom to get back to the data screen.
3. Enter the scores shown above.
4. Save as **PROBF**.
5. Click **Analyze**.
6. Click **Correlate**.
7. Click **Bi Variate**.
8. Click on both variables, **ss** and **lsi**, and put them in the **Variables Box**.
9. Click **Pearson**.
10. Click **two-tailed** and make sure the flag is checked for all **significant correlations**.
11. Click **OK**.

Your screen will look like this:

Correlations

Correlations

		ss	lsi
ss	**Pearson Correlation**	1	.933**
	Sig. (2-tailed)		.000
	N	10	10
lsi	**Pearson Correlation**	.933**	1
	Sig. (2-tailed)	.000	
	N	10	10

** Correlation is significant at the 0.01 level

Conclusion:

A random sample of inmates from a certain state prison was selected and tested on the SS scale, a subtest of the HPSI (Holden Psychological Screening Inventory), and the LSI (Level of Service Inventory). Score on the SS Scale, which measures psychopathy, were compared with scores on the LSI. A Pearson correlation was computed between the scores on the two tests. A strong, positive correlation was found to be 0.933, which is significant at p < .01. Since a strong linear correlation was found, it can be concluded that scores on the SS scale correlated significantly with scores on the LSI, and indicated that an inmate's scores on psychopathy strongly predicted the inmate's level of security risk - the higher the psychopathy scores the greater the risk.

At this point it is instructive to create a scatter plot.

Step-by-Step
1. Click **Graphs** (at the top, just to the right of Analyze) and select **Scatter**.
2. When the scatter plot box appears, check **Simple Scatter** and click **Define**.
3. Now that you see the main scatter plot box, move **LSI** into the **Y axis box**, since that is the dependent variable and move **SS** into the **X axis box**, since that is the independent variable.
4. Click **Titles** and in line 1, type **LSI as a function of SS**.

5. Click **OK** and there it is. In order to see the whole scatter plot, you may have to scroll to the right.

Graph

LSI as a function of SS

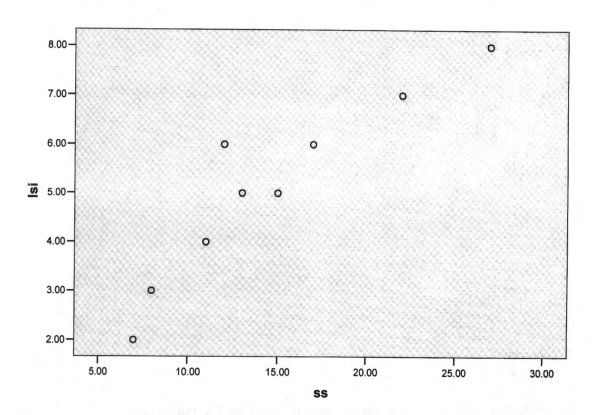

Notice as you examine this scatter plot that the array of data points slopes from lower left to upper right (which is always the case with a positive correlation). Had the correlation been negative, the data points would have sloped from upper left to lower right.

PROBLEM G

Spearman Correlation
With ordinal data or skewed interval data, the Spearman should be chosen as the appropriate correlation tool.

Please use the following example.

A university researcher is interested in discovering if there is a significant relationship between the age of an alum and the amount of money the alum contributed to the college.

Step by Step

1. Click **File**, **New**, and **Data**.
2. Click the **Variable View** tab at the bottom of your screen and when the Variable View screen appears type **donation** in the first row and **age** in the second row. Now click the **Data View** tab at the bottom to get back to the data screen.

Enter the data, which is shown with both variables in rank order (ordinal) form. Notice that since contribution is in rank-order form, subject 3, with a rank of 1 gave the most money and subject 1 with a rank of 12 gave the least. Also note that subject 4 with an age rank of 1 is the oldest. Incidentally, had you had interval scores, such as the exact amount each gave and their actual ages, you wouldn't have to rank order either distribution because, SPSS will rank them for you automatically.

Case	donation	age
1	12	9
2	9	6
3	1	2
4	2	1
5	6	11
6	7	5
7	11	12
8	4	7
9	3	3
10	8	8
11	5	4
12	10	10

Save as PROBG

3. Click **Analyze**.
4. Click **Correlate**.
5. Click **Bivariate**.
6. Move the two variables, **donation** and **age** over into the **Variables box**.
7. Check **Spearman** and toggle off the check at **Pearson**.
8. Click **two-tailed** and check the flag for **significant correlations**.
9. **OK**

SELECTED OUTPUT

Nonparametric Correlations

Correlations

			donation	age
Spearman's rho	donation	Correlation Coefficient	1.000	.790**
		Sig. (2-tailed)	.	.002
		N	12	12
	age	Correlation Coefficient	.790**	1.000
		Sig. (2-tailed)	.002	.
		N	12	12

** Correlation is significant at the 0.01 level (2-tailed).

18

Conclusion:
A Spearman correlation was computed between the amount of money an alum donates to the college and the age of the alum. A strong positive correlation was found (r = .790, p<.01). The correlation was clearly significant and indicates that the older the alum the higher the college contribution.

To show off the ability of SPSS to rank order your scores automatically, assume that for the previous problem we had two distributions of non-normal interval scores.

Case	contribution	age
1	$ 0	25
2	10	30
3	400	80
4	200	90
5	25	23
6	20	35
7	5	22
8	35	28
9	40	55
10	15	26
11	28	40
12	8	24

Now, follow the steps shown above for the Spearman correlation, and your output will be exactly as it was above when you entered the ordinal data directly.

PROBLEM H

One Way ANOVA
This test is used to determine if there are significant differences on the dependent variable scores when **three** or more independent groups have been selected (as opposed to the two-group t ratio). For this problem assume three groups were randomly selected, and the IV was thus manipulated at three levels. Assume further that the dependent variable is based on scores on a certain achievement test.

Step by Step
1. Click **File**, **New**, and **Data**.
2. Click the **Variable View** tab at the bottom of your screen and when the Variable View screen appears type **group** in the first row and **scores** in the second row.
3. Now tab back to the **Data View** screen and rearrange the following data from this

Group 1	Group 2	Group 3
1	2	4
2	3	5
3	4	6

To this: (and enter the data)

Case	scores	group
1	1	1
2	2	1
3	3	1
4	2	2
5	3	2
6	4	2
7	4	3
8	5	3
9	6	3

       Save as **PROBH**
4. Click **Analyze, Compare Means** and **One-Way ANOVA**.
5. Place **scores** as the **Dependent Variable box** and **group** in the **Fixed Factor box**.
6. Click **Options**, and **Homogeneity of Variance** and click **Continue**.
7. Click **Post Hoc** and then **Tukey**.
8. Check **Significance level as .05**.
9. Click **Continue** and **OK**.

SELECTED OUTPUT

Oneway

Test of Homogeneity of Variances

scores

Levene Statistic	df1	df2	Sig.
.000	2	6	1.000

ANOVA

scores

	Sum of squares	df	Mean Square	F	Sig.
Between Groups	14.000	2	7.000	7.000	.027
Within Groups	6.000	6	1.000		
Total	20.000	8			

20

Post Hoc Tests

Multiple Comparisons

Dependent variable: scores
Tukey HSD

(I) group	(J) group	Mean Difference (I–J)	Std. Error	Sig.	95% Confidence Interval Lower Bound	Upper Bound
1.00	2.00	-1.00000	.81650	.483	-3.5052	1.5052
	3.00	-3.00000*	.81650	.024	-5.5052	-.4948
2.00	1.00	1.00000	.81650	.483	-1.5052	3.5052
	3.00	-2.00000	.81650	.109	-4.5052	.5052
3.00	1.00	3.00000*	.81650	.024	.4948	5.5052
	2.00	2.00000	.81650	.109	-.5052	4.5052

* The mean difference is significant at the .05 level.

Homogeneous Subsets

scores

Tukey HSD[a]

group	N	Subset for alpha = .05 1	2
1.00	3	2.0000	
2.00	3	3.0000	3.0000
3.00	3		5.000
Sig.		.483	.109

Means for groups in homogeneous subsets are displayed.
a. Uses Harmonic Mean Sample Size = 3.000.

Here we see the GROUP results, and the F ratio of 7.000, which is significant at the .027 alpha levels. Now check the results of the Levene test (for homogeneity of variance among the groups). Any significance value that is ABOVE .05 indicates homogeneity. In this case the value was at its maximum, 1.000, meaning that the distributions couldn't be more homogeneous. Tukey's HSD, however, tells us that we don't have a difference between Groups 1 and 2 (.483), nor between Groups 2 and 3 (.109), but we do have a significant difference between Groups 1 and 3, (p = .024).

Conclusions:
A one-way ANOVA was computed comparing the scores of subjects who were tested under three different conditions. A significant F ratio was found between the groups, F = 7.000, p<.05). A post-hoc analysis was conducted using Tukey's HSD. Groups 1 and 3 were significantly different, but the other group comparisons were not). The Levene test showed homogeneity of variance among the groups.

PROBLEM I

Factorial ANOVA
The factorial ANOVA is still a univariate analysis, since there is only one dependent variable. Unlike the one-way ANOVA, however, this procedure allows for more than just a single independent variable. Thus, we can select out the main effects for each IV, as well as any possible interactions. Please use the data below for your analysis.

The research in this case is based on testing both diet and exercise (two IVs) and their possible effects on a person's percentage of body fat (the DV).

The body-fat scores are as follows:

	Low fat diet	High fat diet
	10	12
	12	14
Exercise	14	15
	12	16
	10	14
	16	22
	18	24
No	20	24
Exercise	22	22
	20	24

Step by Step

1. Click **File**, **New**, and **Data**.
2. Click the **Variable View** tab at the bottom of your screen and when the Variable View screen appears type **Diet** in the first row, **Exercise** in the second row and **Bodyfat** in the third row. Now click the **Data View** tab at the bottom to get back to the data screen and enter the data as shown below.

Case	diet	exercise	bodyfat
1	1	1	10
2	1	1	12
3	1	1	14
4	1	1	12
5	1	1	10
6	1	2	16
7	1	2	18
8	1	2	20
9	1	2	22
10	1	2	20

Data continue on next page.

22

11	2	1	12
12	2	1	14
13	2	1	15
14	2	1	16
15	2	1	14
16	2	2	22
17	2	2	24
18	2	2	24
19	2	2	22
20	2	2	24

Save as **PROBI**.

3. Click **Analyze**, **General Linear**, and **Univariate**.
4. Enter **bodyfat** as the **Dependent Variable**.
5. Put **diet and exercise** in as **FIXED FACTORS** (the two IVs).
6. Click **Options**, and then move **diet**, **exercise** and **dietexcercise** into **Display Means box**. Also check **Descriptive Statistics** and **Estimate of Effect size**.
7. Check **Continue** and **OK**.

IMPORTANT NOTE

If either of the IVs had been set at more than two levels, then Click Post Hoc, and put whichever IVs are at three or more levels into the "Post Hoc Tests for" box and check Tukey. In this problem we don't need Tukey, because with only two levels of the IVs, the F ratio alone will tell you if there is a significant difference between the scores as a function of the two levels.

SELECTED OUTPUT FOR FACTORIAL ANOVA

This screen gives us all the means, separately and in combination. We get the mean for each treatment condition, as well as the row mean, column mean and overall mean. We are also given all the standard deviation combinations.

Univariate Analysis of Variance

Between-Subjects Factors

		N
diet	1.00	10
	2.00	10
exercise	1.00	10
	2.00	10

23

Descriptive Statistics

Dependent Variable: bodyfat

diet	exercise	Mean	Std. Deviation	N
1.00	1.00	11.6000	1.67332	5
	2.00	19.2000	2.28035	5
	Total	15.4000	4.42719	10
2.00	1.00	14.2000	1.48324	5
	2.00	23.2000	1.09545	5
	Total	18.7000	4.90011	10
Total	1.00	12.9000	2.02485	10
	2.00	21.2000	2.69979	10
	Total	17.0500	4.85012	20

This next table provides the heart of the analysis. We interpret the F ratios for the two main effects, DIET (F=19.105) and EXERCISE (F=120.860), as well as for the interaction, TEMP*EXERCISE (F=0.860).

Tests of Between-Subjects Effects

Dependent Variable: bodyfat

Source	Type III Sum of Squares	df	Mean Square	F	Sig.	Partial Eta Squared
Corrected Model	401.350[a]	3	133.783	46.942	.000	.898
Intercept	5814.050	3	5814.050	2040.018	.000	.992
diet	54.450	1	54.450	19.105	.000	.544
exercise	344.450	1	344.450	120.860	.000	.883
diet * exercise	2.450	1	2.450	.860	.368	.051
Error	45.600	16	2.850			
Total	6261.000	20				
Corrected Total	446.950	19				

a. R Squared = .898 (Adjusted R Squared = .879)

Conclusions:

A 2 x 2 between subjects factorial ANOVA was conducted in an attempt to discover possible differences in body-fat scores as a function of the two independent variables, diet and exercise. A significant main effect for diet was found (F(1,16)=19.105, p<.01), as well as a significant main effect for exercise (F(1,16)=120.860, p<.01). The low-fat diet produced less body fat than the High-fat diet, and Exercise produced less body fat than the no exercise condition. There was no significant interaction effect (F(1,16)=0.860, p>.05). The main effects were NOT significantly influenced by each other.

Graphing the Results

To use SPSS for graphing your results, follow the procedure shown previously, but this time when you get to step 5 Click **Continue** and then INSTEAD OF OK, click **Plots** and move **exercise** into the **horizontal box** (because it was in the rows, which are horizontal), and move **Diet** into the **Separate Lines box**. Click **Add, Continue** and **OK**, and there's your graph.

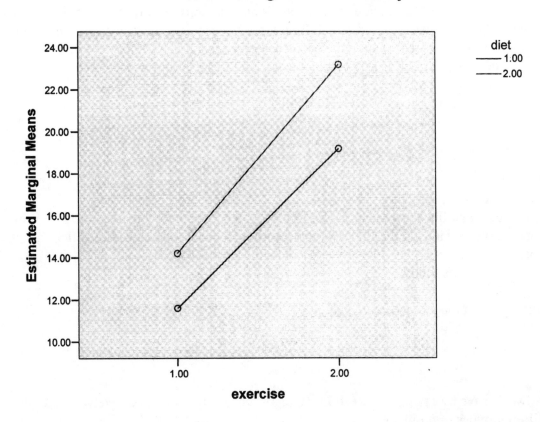

Estimated Marginal Means of bodyfat

PROBLEM J

Chi Square

We will first cover the 1 by k Chi Square, also called Goodness of Fit. This test is used on nominal or categorical data to establish whether frequency differences have occurred on the basis of chance. The 1 by k Chi Square is used when one group is sorted into any number of categories.

Problem J1

To illustrate the 1 by k Chi Square we will assess how persons view crime in their city. A sample 100 urban adults was selected and asked if they thought crime in their city was "more serious," "the same" or "less serious" than in the past (the "past" as a time period was left purposefully vague). Code More Serious as a 1, The Same as 2 and Less Serious as a 3.

More Serious	The Same	Less Serious
150	100	50

Step by Step

1. Click **File**, **New**, and **Data**.
2. Click the **Variable View** tab at the bottom of your screen and when the Variable View screen appears type **serious** in the first row and **number** in the second row. Now click the tab at the bottom called **Data View** to get back to the data screen.
3. Enter the data as follows:

Serious	number
1	150
2	100
3	50

   Now file save by saving as **PROBJ1**. (Use J1 because for chi-square we will be doing two different types of problems).
4. Click **data** and **weight cases**.
5. The next screen asks whether to weight cases, and you should check the second option, which says **weight cases by**.
6. Click **number** and move it into the **Frequency Variable box**.
7. Click **OK**.
8. Click **Analyze** and **Nonparametric Tests**.
9. Click **Chi Square**, and put **serious** in the **Test Variable List** and check **All Categories equal**.
10. **OK**

SELECTED OUTPUT

Chi-Square Test

Frequencies

serious

	Observed N	Expected N	Residual
1.00	150	100.00	50.0
2.00	100	100.0	.0
3.00	300		
Total	300		

Test Statistics

	serious
Chi-Square[a]	50.000
df	2
Asymp. Sig.	.000

a. 0 cells (.0%) have expected frequencies less than 5. The minimum expected cell frequency is 100.0.

Conclusions:
A 1 by k goodness-of-fit Chi Square was computed comparing the frequency of occurrence of a sample of urban adults according to three opinion categories toward crime in their city, "More Serious", "The Same" or "Less Serious" than in the past. A significant difference was found between the observed and expected values (chi-square(2) = 50.000, p < .01.). The urban adults viewed crime as significantly more serious than in the recent past. (Results such as these are common in the urban population, even in those areas where the crime rate has fallen).

Problem J 2
The r by k Chi Square is used on nominal data in situations when two or more groups have been sorted into any number of categories. For this test, please use the following data:

A researcher wants to discover whether involvement in a treatment program reduced the number of drug-abuse inmates who recidivated. For this analysis we will use both the Chi Square as well as the Coefficient of Contingency, which is a nominal measure of both correlation and effect size).

The 2 by 2 contingency table is as follows:

	Recidivated		
	Yes	No	Total
Treatment Program	30	70	100
No Treatment	62	38	100

27

Step by Step

1. Click **File**, **New**, and **Data**.
2. Click the **Variable View** tab at the bottom of your screen and when the Variable View screen appears type **treat** in the first row, **recid** in the second, and **number** in the third row. Now click the **Data View** tab at the bottom and get back to the data screen. Notice that the number 30 is in treat row 1 and recid in column 1. The number 70 is in treatment row 1, but is in recid column 2 and so on. Now enter the data as follow:

treat	recid	number
1	1	30
1	2	70
2	1	62
2	2	38

Save as **PROBJ2**.

3. Click **Data** and then select **Weight Cases** (at the bottom of the menu).
4. Click **weight cases by** and then check the **weight cases by** option.
5. Move **number** into the **Frequency Variable box** and **OK**.
6. Click **Analyze**, **Descriptives** and **Crosstabs**.
7. Put **treat** in rows and **recid** in columns.
8. Click **statistics** and then check both **Chi Square** and **C**, the coefficient of contingency.
9. Click **Continue** and **OK**.

Selected Output

Chi-Square Tests

	Value	df	Asymp. Sig. (2-sided)	Exact Sig. (2-sided)	Exact Sig. (1-sided)
Pearson Chi-Square	20.612[b]	1	.000		
Continuity Correction[a]	19.344	1	.000		
Likelihood Ratio	20.992	1	.000		
Fisher's Exact Test				.000	.000
Linear-by-Linear Association	20.509	1	.000		
N of Valid Cases	200				

a. computed only for a 2x2 table
b. 0 cells (.0%) have expected count less than 5. The minimum expected count is 46.00.

Symmetric Measures

		Value	Approx. Sig.
Nominal by Nominal	Contingency Coefficient	.306	.000
N of Valid Cases		200	

a. Not assuming the null hypothesis.
b. Using the asymptotic standard error assuming the null hypothesis.

Conclusions:

A 2 by 2 chi-square was computed comparing the frequency of recidivism between inmates who had received treatment and those who had not. A significant difference was found between the two groups (chi-square(1) = 20.612, p<.01). (Had the Chi-Square been used to test for correlation, the C (Contingency Coefficient) of .306 would then be included). Using the C value for effect size we note that a value of .306 indicates a medium effect size.

PROBLEM K

Multiple Regression

This test is used to make predictions on one y variable (DV) on the basis of two or more x variables (IVs). The data for this problem comes from testing 20 subjects on the Eysenck Personality Test, and the letters ES, S and V refer to, ES=Experience Seeking, S=Sociability and V=Venturesomeness.

Step by Step

1. Click **File, New,** and **Data**.
2. Click the **Variable View** tab at the bottom of your screen and when the Variable View screen appears type in **es** in the first row, **s** in the second row and **v** in the third row. Now click the **Data View** tab at the bottom to get back to the data screen.

For this example, we are going to predict V (venturesomeness) as the dependent variable.

Case	es	s	v
1	16	5	8
2	19	6	8
3	15	7	7
4	15	6	8
5	14	5	6
6	15	6	8
7	13	6	7
8	12	6	8
9	4	6	2
10	15	8	7
11	16	4	7
12	14	5	7
13	17	6	8
14	13	7	10
15	14	2	4
16	15	7	12
17	17	5	4
18	26	14	17
19	16	5	8
20	14	6	7

Save as **PROBK**.
3. Click **Analyze**, **Regression**, and **Linear**.
4. Click **v** (since that is the variable being predicted) and put in as the **Dependent Variable**.
5. Click **es** and put it in as the **first Independent Variable**.
6. Click **s** and put it in as the **second Independent Variable**.
7. Click **Statistics** – at the bottom middle of the screen and click **Keep Estimates, Model Fit** and **Descriptives**.
8. Click **Continue** and **OK**.

SELECTED OUTPUT

Regression

Descriptive Statistics

	Mean	Std. Deviation	N
v	7.6500	3.04830	20
es	15.0000	3.90681	20
s	6.1000	2.24546	20

Correlations

		v	es	s
Pearson Correlation	v	1.000	.716	.774
	es	.716	1.000	.516
	s	.774	.516	1.000
Sig. (1-tailed)	v	.	.000	.000
	es	.000	.	.010
	s	.000	.010	.
N	v	20	20	20
	es	20	20	20
	s	20	20	20

Variables Entered/Removed[b]

Model	Variables Entered	Variables Removed	Method
1	s, es[a]	.	Enter

a. All requested variables entered.

b. Dependent Variable: v

Model Summary

Model	R	R Square	Adjusted R Square	Std. Error of the Estimate
1	.858[a]	.736	.705	1.65578

a. Predictors: (Constant), s, es

ANOVA[b]

Model		Sum of Squares	df	Mean Square	F	Sig.
1	Regression	129.943	2	64.971	23.698	.000[a]
	Residual	46.607	17	2.742		
	Total	176.550	19			

a. Predictors: (Constant), s, es

Coefficients[a]

Model		Unstandardized Coefficients		Standardized Coefficients	t	Sig.
		B	Std. Error	Beta		
1	(Constant)	-1.967	1.540		-1.277	.219
	es	.336	.114	.431	2.964	.009
	s	.749	.197	.552	3.793	.001

a. Dependent Variable: v

31

Notice that the output gives us SIX important tables. First we get Descriptives, showing the means and standard deviations for all three variables. Then we get the matrix of internal correlations, showing the Pearson r relationships among the three variables, V, ES and S. Then, under Variables Entered/Removed, we find that both s and es were entered and none were removed. Under Model Summary, we get both the multiple R (.858) and R square (.736). Then, finally, under ANOVA, we get the significance of the multiple R (which with an F value of 23.698 is clearly significant at p<.01, and under coefficients we get the regression equation. The constant of -1.967 is the a value or intercept, and the B values are the slopes, or the weights associated with the regression equation. Thus, the regression equation is read as follows.

Ymult pred = .336 + .749 -1.967

This is the equation for predicting V values on the basis of ES and S scores. The Beta values are the standardized weights (based on a mean of 0 and an SD of 1.00) and indicate the relative importance of the independent variables. Notice in this case that S was a stronger predictor, .552, than ES, .431. The t values give the significance levels of the weights.

Conclusions:
A multiple linear correlation was computed to predict V (Venturesomeness) from both ES (Experience Seeking) and S (Sociability). The R was found to be .858, and was significant $(F(2,17) = 23.698, p<.01)$. The linear combination of ES and S was a significant predictor of V.

PROBLEM L

Partial Correlation
This test allows for the possibility of ruling out the effects of one or more variables (the variables being partialled out) on the relationship among the remaining variables. The problem to be addressed here involves evaluating the correlation between reading speed (rs) and reading comprehension (comp), with the influence of IQ being partialled out (or statistically controlled.)

Step by Step
1. Click **File**, **New**, and **Data**.
2. Click the **Variable View** tab at the bottom of your screen and when the Variable View screen appears type in **rs** in the first row, **comp** in the second, and **iq** in the third row.
3. Now click the **Data View** tab at the bottom to get back to the data screen.

Enter the data as follows:

rs	comp	iq
55	50	100
35	45	95
75	60	135
30	40	90
45	50	105
50	45	100
45	40	95
55	60	110
48	52	102
42	48	100

Save as PROBL

4. Click **Analyze**.
5. Click **Correlate**.
6. Click **Partial** and put **rs** and **comp** in the **Variables box** and **iq** in the **Controlling for box**.
7. Check **Two-tailed** and **Display actual significance levels**.
8. **OK**.

Selected Output

Partial Corr

Correlations

Control Variables			rs	comp
iq	rs	Correlation	1.000	.125
		Significance (2-tailed)	.	.749
		df	0	7
	comp	Correlation	.125	1.000
		Significance (2-tailed)	.749	.
		df	7	0

Conclusions:

A partial correlation coefficient was computed between Reading Speed and Reading Comprehension with the IQ variable being partialled out. The resulting correlation = .125, (p = .749) was not significant. The two variables, Reading Speed and Reading Comprehension, are independent of each other when the IQ variable is statistically controlled. The above p value of .749 shows the significance level to be FAR above .05, so high as to indicate the chance of alpha error as being almost 80%. Finally, it would be instructive if you were to run a Pearson correlation (the procedure for which was shown previously) between reading speed (rs) and comprehension (comp). You will find that the correlation is .785, which is significant at .008. Thus, when IQ was controlled for, that strong and highly significant correlation virtually disappeared.

PROBLEM M

Paired t

The paired t evaluates the hypothesis of difference between two sample means when the sample selections have not been independent. This test requires interval or ratio data (called Scale by SPSS) and is typically used in before-after or matched-group designs. Please use the data shown below. These data are based on a before-after study of the possible effects of weapon design on shooting accuracy. A group of officers was randomly selected from a large, metropolitan police force and brought to the firing range. First, all subjects used their traditionally issued service revolvers, and their error scores (in inches from the bull's-eye) were recorded. Then they all fired again using the newly-designed polymer pistols and their error scores were again determined. Notice that as was the case with the Pearson r (previously shown), scores are listed side by side.

Step by Step

1. Click **File**, **New**, and **Data**.
2. Click the **Variable View** tab at the bottom of your screen and when the Variable View screen appears type in **pre** in the first row and **post** in the second row. Now click the **Data View** tab at the bottom and get back to the data screen.
3. Then enter the measures

Case	pre	post
1	3	2
2	5	3
3	7	5
4	5	3
5	10	6
6	2	0
7	6	2
8	3	1
9	1	1
10	0	0

Save as PROBM

4. Click **Analyze** and **Compare Means**.
5. Click **Paired Samples t test**.
6. Click **pre** and **post** and put them both into the **paired variables** box.
7. **OK**

SELECTED OUTPUT

T-Test

Paired Samples Statistics

		Mean	N	Std. Deviation	Std. Error Mean
Pair 1	pre	4.2000	10	3.01109	.95219
	post	2.3000	10	2.00278	.63333

Paired Samples Correlations

		N	Correlation	Sig.
Pair 1	pre & post	10	.929	.000

Paired Samples Test

		Paired Differences					
				Std. Error	95% Confidence Interval of the Difference		
		Mean	Std. Deviation	Mean	Lower	Upper	t
Pair 1	pre – post	1.90000	1.37032	.43333	.91973	2.88027	4.385

Paired Samples Test

		df	Sig. (2-tailed)
Pair 1	pre-post	9	.002

Conclusion:

The paired t was computed on this pre-post study. The Pearson r correlation was found to be significant (r(8) = .929, p<.01). The paired t was significant (t(9) = 4.385, p <.05). The scores were significantly lower in the posttest, showing that shooting accuracy did improve with the use of the new weapon.

Caution: Before concluding that it was definitely the independent variable (new weapon) that produced the change, we must look at the internal validity of this study. It may be that scores might improve the second time simply as a result of having had a practice round. This could confound the independent variable. It would be better to have another group in which the new weapon was used in the pre test and the old weapon used in the post test. We might even have a third group that used the old weapon twice, and perhaps even a fourth group where the new weapon was used twice.

PROBLEM N

Within-Subjects (Repeated Measure ANOVA)

The within-subjects ANOVA is used to test the hypothesis of difference on interval scores when the sample selection has not been independent (as was the case with the paired t). However with this test you can evaluate several sample means (not just two). It is typically used in repeated-measure designs.

Please use the following example: A researcher attempted to find out whether buying TV time for repeated showing of a political propaganda film is worth the cost. That is, do people's attitudes change more the more times they see the film? An experiment was designed in which a sample of registered voters was asked to complete an "Attitude Toward the Candidate" questionnaire (high scores indicate a pro attitude). They see the film three times and fill out the questionnaire after each showing.

Step by Step

1. Click **File**, **New**, and **Data**.
2. Click the **Variable View** tab at the bottom of your screen and when the Variable View screen appears type **first** in the first row, **second** in the second row, and **third** in the third row. Now click back to the **Data View** tab at the bottom to find the data screen.
3. Enter data.

Case	first	second	third
1	1	2	3
2	2	4	6
3	3	3	3
4	4	5	6
5	5	6	7

      Save as PROBN

4. Click **Analyze**.
5. Click **General Linear**.
6. Click **GLM repeated measures**.
7. Type **time** in **Factor Name** and **3** in **number of levels**.
8. Click **ADD**, and **Define**. Then click on **first, second, third**, and move them to the **Within Subjects box**.
9. Click **Options** and then **Descriptive statistics**.
10. Click **Continue** and **OK**

IMPORTANT NOTE:

If your version of SPSS does not have "GLM Repeated Measures", go to your computer lab and inquire as to whether the full version of SPSS is available to you. If so, you will be able to complete the preceding problem in the lab.

SELECTED OUTPUT

This shows us the means and standard deviations for each of the time periods

Descriptive Statistics

	Mean	Std. Deviation	N
first	3.0000	1.58114	5
second	4.0000	1.58114	5
third	5.0000	1.87083	5

This gives us the F ratio and its significance, which can be read as .007.

Tests of Within-Subjects Effects

Measure: MEASURE_1

Source		Type III Sum of Squares	df	Mean Square	F	Sig.
time	Sphericity Assumed	10.000	2	5.000	10.000	.007
	Greenhouse-Geisser	10.000	1.000	10.000	10.000	.034
	Huynh-Feldt	10.000	1.000	10.000	10.000	.034
	Lower-bound	10.000	1.000	10.000	10.000	.034
Error (time)	Sphericity Assumed	4.000	8	.5000		
	Greenhouse-Geisser	4.000	4.000	1.000		
	Huynh-Feldt	4.000	4.000	1.000		
	Lower-bound	4.000	4.000	1.000		

Sphericity is a term used in within-subjects ANOVAs to indicate that the variances of the differences for the paired measures are fairly equal. That is, it tests for the homogeneity of the covariance. Unless this assumption is met, the within-subjects F ratio may lead to ambiguous results. SPSS uses the Mauchly W test to determine sphericity, and it shows that the covariance is homogeneous whenever the p value is GREATER than .05. For this problem we can assume sphericity and read the p value for our F ratio as .007. If the Mauchly had led to a p value of less than .05, then you would read the F ratio as .034 (the Greenhouse-Geisser value) which is still significant. You really don't have to be concerned by the SPSS explanation that sphericity tests the hypothesis that "the error covariance matrix of the orthonormalized transformed dependent variables are proportional to an identity matrix". Try that phrase over lunch tomorrow and watch the room clear.

Conclusions:
A one-way within-subjects ANOVA was computed, comparing political attitudes for subjects at three different times, after viewing a propaganda film once, then after seeing it again, and finally after viewing it for a third time. A significant F ratio was found ($F_{(2,8)} = 10.000$, $p < .01$). As the film was repeatedly shown, the subjects' attitudes became increasingly positive. The researcher concluded that it was to the candidate's benefit to keep showing the same film over and over.

THE ORDINAL TESTS

PROBLEM O

The Mann-Whitney Test U Test

This is a test of the hypothesis of difference between two independently selected groups that have been measured using ordinal (ranked) data. It is the equivalent of the independent t when ordinal data are used instead of interval. For this problem we are going to compare a sample of law-abiding citizens with a sample of ex-convicts on each individual's yearly income. For this problem call the Citizens Group1 and the Ex-Cons Group2.

Step by Step

1. Click **File**, **New**, and **Data**.
2. Click the **Variable View** tab at the bottom of your screen and when the Variable View screen appears type **ranks** in the first row, and **group** in the second row. Now click the **Data View** tab at the bottom to get back to the data screen. Remember, these are ordinal data, which means that in the income column a rank of 1 indicates the highest income and a rank of 21 is the lowest. (The citizens are in group 1 and the ex-cons in group2).
3. Line the data up as follows:

ranks	group
8	1
7	1
5	1
6	1
1	1
4	1
3	1
2	1
14	1
15	1
21	2
20	2
19	2
18	2
9	2
10	2
11	2
12	2
13	2
16	2
17	2

Save as **PROBO**

4. Click **Analyze**.
5. Click. **Nonparametrics**.
6. Click **2 Independent Samples**.
7. Put **income** in for the **Test Variable** and **group** in the **Grouping Variable box**.
8. Click **Mann-Whitney**.
9. Click **Define Variables**, and type a **1** for **Group1** and a **2** for **Group2**.
10. Click **Continue** and **OK**.

SELECTED OUTPUT

NPar Tests

Mann–Whitney Test

Ranks

	group	N	Mean Rank	Sum of Ranks
income	1.00	10	6.50	65.00
	2.00	11	15.09	166.00
	Total	21		

Test Statistics[b]

	income
Mann-Whitney U	10.000
Wilcoxon W	65.000
Z	-3.169
Asymp. Sig. (2-tailed)	.002
Exact Sig. [2*(1-tailed Sig.)]	.001[a]

a. Not corrected for ties.
b. Grouping Variable: group

The Mann-Whitney test is based on the resulting Z value of -3.169. The sign of the Z tells us that the mean rank in Group 1 is lower than the mean rank in Group 2, which means Group 1 is wealthier. Remember that with ordinal data low NUMERICAL ranks mean higher scores. Ranks of 1 and 2 stand for the first and second places, whereas a rank of 21 (as in the above case) resulted from being in LAST place.

Conclusions:
A Mann-Whitney test was computed to test for the difference in income levels between law-abiding citizens and ex-convicts. The law-abiding citizens earned more, ranked lower in ordinal terms, with a mean rank of 6.50 compared to the ex-con's higher mean rank of 15.09. The analysis showed a significant difference ($z = -3.169$, $p < .001$). It may very well be that those individuals who had served prison time may not have been afforded the opportunity to interview for higher paying jobs.

PROBLEM P

Kruskal–Wallis H Test
The H test is a test of the hypothesis of difference on ordinal data among at least three independently selected samples. The Kruskal-Wallis can be thought of as the ordinal counterpart of the one-way ANOVA. Suppose the Federal Aviation Administration is interested in whether flying ability is a function of the pilot's age. A sample of 24 licensed pilots was selected, with 6 pilots from each age group. Group 1 consists of ages 21 to 30. In Group two the pilots are between 31 and 40 and in Group 3 they are between 41 and 50, and finally in Group 4 they are between 51 and 60.

Step by Step
1. Click **File**, **New**, and **Data**.
2. Click the **Variable View** tab at the bottom of your screen and when the Variable View screen appears type **Ranks** in the first row and **Group** in the second row. Now click the **Data View** tab to get back to the data screen. Enter the data below. The data have been set up in groups so that the 21–30 ages are in Group 1, the 31–40s in Group 2, the 41–50s in Group 3 and the 51–60s in Group 4.

Ranks	Group
2	1
4	1
18	1
1	1
3	1
7	1
20	2
6	2
8	2
5	2
9	2
12	2
23	3
11	3
15	3
13	3
10	3
14	3
24	4
17	4
22	4
21	4
19	4
16	4

Save as PROBP

40

3. Click **Analyze**.
4. Click **Nonparametrics**.
5. Click **K Independent Samples and check Kruskal-Wallis H**.
6. Put **Rank** in the **Test Variable List** and **Group** in as the **Grouping Variable**.
7. Click **Define Range** and type **1** for **Minimum** and **4** for **Maximum**.
8. Click **Continue** and **OK**.

Selected Output

NPar Tests

Kruskal–Wallis Test

Ranks

	group	N	Mean Rank
ranks	1.00	6	5.83
	2.00	6	10.00
	3.00	6	14.33
	4.00	6	19.83
	Total	24	

As the output shows, the Kruskal-Wallis H value was a significant 12.940, $p < .01$.

Conclusions:
A Kruskal-Wallis test was performed on pilot ratings based on age. The differences were significant, with the younger pilots receiving significantly higher ratings than was the case for the older pilots ($H (3) = 12.940$, $p < .01$).

41

PROBLEM Q

Wilcoxon T
This is an ordinal test of the hypothesis of difference when the samples are correlated, as in the case of before-after or matched-group designs. The Wilcoxon T is the ordinal counterpart of the paired t.

The data to be used come from a matched-group design where the subjects have been paired off on a relevant variable. In this case a golf pro has created a new teaching method, including videotape replays. A random sample of golfers at a certain country club was selected and placed into MATCHED groups based on their average scores. The subjects in the experimental group are then given a solid week's training in the new method, while those in the control group are taught in the traditional way. In looking over the golf scores it was discovered the distributions were badly skewed, since in each group there were some duffers who had extremely high scores. Remember that in golf, high scores are not Tiger Woods scores. To compensate for the skew, it was decided to take the interval golf scores and convert them down to ordinal and use a non-parametric analysis – hence the Wilcoxon T.

Step by Step
1. Click **File**, **New**, and **Data**.
2. Click the **Variable View** tab at the bottom of your screen and when the Variable View screen appears type in **pair#** in the first row, **Exscore** (for the experimental group scores), and **Conscore** (for the control group scores). Now click the **Data View** tab at the bottom to get back to the data screen.

   Enter the data as follows:

pair#	exscore	conscore
1	85	86
2	90	95
3	92	96
4	93	93
5	93	95
6	94	96
7	95	98
8	95	101
9	140	133
10	150	135

   Save as **PROBQ**
3. Click **Analyze**.
4. Click **Nonparametrics**, and then **2 Related Samples**.
5. Put BOTH **exscore** and **conscore** into the **Test Pairs List**.
6. Click **Wilcoxon**.
7. Click **OK**.

NPar Tests

Wilcoxon Signed Ranks Test

Ranks

		N	Mean Rank	Sum of Ranks
conscore - exscore	Negative Ranks	2[a]	8.50	17.00
	Positive Ranks	7[b]	4.00	28.00
	Ties	1[c]		
	Total	10		

a. conscore < exscore
b. conscore > exscore
c. conscore = exscore

Test Statistics[b]

	conscore - exscore
Z	-.652a
Asymp. Sig. (2-tailed	.514

a. Based on negative ranks
b. Wilcoxon Signed Ranks Test

With a p value of greater than .05, the Z value of -.652 did not reach significance.

CONCLUSIONS:

A Wilcoxon T test was computed on the scores of matched groups of golfers, one group having had special training and the other with traditional training. No significant differences were found (Z = -.652, p > .05). In short, the special golf training with videotaping did not work any better than the traditional training.

PROBLEM R

Friedman ANOVA

The Friedman is a test of the hypothesis of difference on ordinal or skewed interval data when either the sample groups have been matched, or a single sample has been repeatedly measured. The Friedman is the ordinal equivalent of the within subjects F ratio (ANOVA) when there are interval data. Assume that a researcher wants to find out if there are LSI differences among incarcerated inmates according to their number of previous incarcerations. The LSI (Level of Security Index) measures the security threat an inmate might pose while in custody. Inmate samples from each category were selected and MATCHED on the basis of IQ (since both the LSI and number of prior commitments might be influenced by intelligence. Then the matched trios are all categorized on the basis of previous incarcerations, 1 (no previous incarcerations), 2 (1 to 3 previous incarcerations), or 3 (more than 3 previous incarcerations). They were then rank ordered on the basis of their LSI scores. Since this particular LSI distribution was so badly skewed, it was decided to convert the scores to ordinal form, with 1 being the highest, 2 the next highest and 3 the lowest.

Step by Step
1. Click **File**, **New**, and **Data**.
2. Click the **Variable View** tab at the bottom of your screen and when the Variable View screen appears type **triad** (threesome) in the first row, **group1** (for no previous in the second row, **group2** (for 1 to 3 previous) in the third row and **group3** (for more than 3 previous) in the fourth row. Now click the **Data View** tab at the bottom to get back to the data screen.

Type the LSI Score ranks as follows:

triad	group1	group2	group3
1	2	1	3
2	2	1	3
3	2	1	3
4	1	2	3
5	2	3	1
6	3	2	1
7	3	1	2
8	1	2	3
9	3	2	1
10	2	3	1

Save as **PROBR**.

3. Click **Analyze**.
4. Click **Nonparametrics**.
5. Click **K Related Samples**.
6. Put all three groups into the **Test Variables box**.
7. Click **Friedman**.
8. Click **OK**.

Selected Output.

Friedman Test

Ranks

	Mean Rank
group1	2.10
group2	1.80
group3	2.10

Test Statistics[a]

N	10
Chi-Square	.600
df	2
Asymp. Sig.	.741

a. Friedman Test

Chi Square is equal to .600, which as can be seen above is NOT significant (p > .05).

Conclusions:
The Friedman ANOVA by ranks was used to assess whether LSI (Level of Security) scores differ as a function of the number of prior incarcerations among a population of prison inmates. Because intelligence may be an influencing factor on both LSI scores and previous incarcerations inmate triads were matched on IQ. The results were not significant (Chi-Square (2) = .600, p>.05). When inmates were matched on IQ, LSI scores did not separate the groups according to the number of previous incarcerations.

PROBLEM S

Reliability

Problem S1
In this section on reliability, there will be three different problems, labeled S1, S2 and S3. These problems will all be focusing on test reliability and will cover the three main types, test-retest reliability, split-half reliability and the use of coefficient alpha as a measure of internal consistency and item analysis.

For the first reliability problem, test-retest, use the data shown below in which the reliability of the figure-ground test is to be assessed. Since this is a test-retest analysis, use the procedure for the Pearson r.

Step by Step
1. Click **File**, **New**, and **Data**.
2. Click the **Variable View** tab at the bottom of your screen and when the Variable View screen appears type in **test** in the first row and **retest** in the second row. Now click the **Data View** tab at the bottom to get back to the data screen.

3. Enter the scores as follows:

Case	test	retest
1	15	16
2	12	15
3	11	12
4	20	22
5	14	18
6	16	15
7	17	15
8	16	17
9	9	9
10	20	21

Save as **PROBS1**.

4. Click **Analyze**.
5. Click **Correlation**.
6. Click **Bivariate**.
7. Click on both variables, **test** and **retest**, and put them BOTH in the **Variables Box**.
8. Click **Pearson**.
9. Click **OK**.

Selected Output

Correlations

Correlations

		test	retest
test	Pearson Correlation	1	.891**
	Sig. (2-tailed)		.001
	N	10	10
retest	Pearson Correlation	.891**	1
	Sig. (2-tailed)	.001	
	N	10	10

** Correlation is significant at the 0.01 level

Here we find the Pearson r, which is the appropriate statistical test for a test-retest analysis with interval data. The r value of .891 is significant, with a p of only .001.

Conclusions

The reliability of this test was assessed using the test-retest method. The Pearson r resulted in a value of .891, which is significant at a p of < .01. The test is clearly reliable and has now been proven to provide consistent results.

PROBLEM S2

Split Half Reliability

With this method, the test to be analyzed is split in half, usually odd items versus even items. In this way only one administration of the test is needed. To correct for splitting the test into two parts, the Spearman-Brown formula is used to establish what the reliability of the entire test should be. For this analysis, use the data shown below where a split-half reliability is being calculated. With SPSS, you don't have to compute the original Pearson r and then correct it. Instead you can go directly to the Corrected Spearman-Brown value.

Step by Step

1. Click **File**, **New**, and **Data**.
2. Click the **Variable View** tab at the bottom of your screen and when the Variable View screen appears type **odd** in the first row and **even** in the second row. Now click the **Data View** tab at the bottom to get back to the data screen.
3. Enter the scores as follows:

Case	odd	even
1	125	120
2	100	100
3	75	80
4	90	95
5	110	105
6	95	90
7	105	110
8	97	98
9	103	102
10	100	100

Save as **PROBS2**.

4. Click **Analyze**.
5. Click **Scale**.
6. Click **Reliability**.
7. Click on both variables, **odd** and **even**, and put them BOTH in the **Variables Box**.
8. Go to the pull-down menu next to "model" and move down to **Split Half**.
9. Click **Split Half** and **OK**.

SELECTED OUTPUT

Reliability Statistics

Cronbach's Alpha	Part 1	Value	1.000
		N of Items	1[a]
	Part 2	Value	1.000
		N of items	1[b]
	Total N of Items		2
Correlation Between Forms			.956
Spearman-Brown	Equal Length		.978
Coefficient	Unequal Length		.978
Guttman Split-Half Coefficient			.970

a. The items are: odd, odd.
b. The items are: even, even.

Conclusions

The reliability of this test was assessed using the split-half method. The Spearman-Brown equal-length value computed to .978. The test is clearly reliable and has now been proven to provide consistent results.

Problem S3

Item Analysis: Coefficient Alpha

For an internal consistency reliability model, we have chosen Cronbach's Alpha. Actually, Cronbach's alpha will give precisely the same value as will the Cyril Hoyt. Alpha has the advantage, however, of identifying which items are or are not contributing to the overall reliability. Without a computer program, it can be very labor-intensive to calculate, but with SPSS it takes only a few seconds (once the data are entered). For this example, use the following data, based on a study of five randomly selected subjects on scores from a 4-item test.

Step by Step

1. Click **File**, **New**, and **Data**.
2. Click the **Variable View** tab at the bottom of your screen and when the Variable View screen appears type in **itema** (for item a) in the first row, **itemb** in the second, so on down to **itemd**.
3. Then click the tab back to the **Data View** screen and enter the scores as shown below.

CASE	itema	itemb	itemc	itemd
1	6	6	5	4
2	4	6	5	3
3	4	4	4	2
4	3	1	4	2
5	1	2	1	1

Save as **PROBS3**.

4. Click **Analyze** then **Scale**.

5. Click **Reliability Analysis**.
6. Move all four items (**itema, itemb, itemc** and **itemd**) into the **Items box**.
7. Click **Alpha** and **OK**.

Selected Output

Reliability Statistics

Cronbach's Alpha	N of Items
.920	4

CONCLUSIONS:
The reliability of this test was measured on the basis of Cronbach's Coefficient Alpha. This internal consistency measure was computed out to be .920, indicating a very high degree of internal reliability.

PROBLEM T

Validity
Test validity attempts to assess whether the test is really measuring what it purports to measure. That is, if a test is supposed to be measuring something like sociability, a valid test will be measuring just that, and not some other extraneous variable(s), like penmanhip. Before a test is evaluated for validity, it first must be shown to be reliable. For this problem, we will use data based on a sample of subjects being tested on a personality trait called Sociability. In this example the subjects' scores on a test of Sociability were compared with the observer's (the judge's) ranking of the subject's perceived sociability in a one-hour group situation.

Step by Step
1. Click **File**, **New**, and **Data**.
2. Click the **Variable View** tab at the bottom of your screen and when the Variable View screen appears type in **ranks1** (for the score ranks) in the first row and ranks2 (for the judge's ranks) in the second row.
3. Now click the **Data View** tab at the bottom to get back to the data screen.
4. Enter the scores as follows:

CASE	ranks1	ranks2
1	2	3
2	10	9
3	8	10
4	3	5
5	9	7
6	1	1
7	6	2
8	7	8
9	4	6
10	5	4

Save as **PROBT**.

5. Click **Analyze**.
6. **Correlation**.
7. **Bi Variate**.
8. Click on both variables, **ranks1** and **ranks2**, and put them in the **Variables Box**.
9. Blank out the **Pearson** box and click on the **Spearman box**.
10. Click **OK**.

SELECTED OUTPUT

Nonparametric Correlations

Correlations

			ranks1	ranks2
Spearman's rho	ranks1	Correlation Coefficient	1.000	.782**
		Sig. (2-tailed)		.008
		N	10	10
	ranks2	Correlation Coefficient	.782**	1.000
		Sig. (2-tailed)	.008	
		N	10	10

** Correlation is significant at the 0.01 level (2-tailed).

Conclusions:

A Spearman correlation was run on a test of Sociability to assess its validity. The test scores were correlated with the rankings of judges who observed all the subjects in a one-hour social situation. Since the scores of the judges were in ordinal form, the test scores were previously converted to ordinal and the Spearman was computed. The Spearman value of .782 was significant at the .008 level. Based on these data the test is statistically valid.

Advanced Inferential Techniques

Although the following statistical procedures are not always covered in the first statistics course, you may find a need for them in your experimental psychology or your criminal justice research methods courses.

PROBLEM U

ANCOVA – Analysis of Covariance
When experimental control of a key variable is impossible (which occurs when you can't get subjects who are alike on such variables as age, gender or IQ) it's still possible to apply a statistical control (as opposed to an experimental control) by using a covariance analysis. For example, a researcher wants to know if math aptitude might influence the results of three different methods of teaching math. In this study, then, math aptitude will be the covariate, the three teaching methods will be the IV, and scores on a math achievement test will be the DV. We will use 6 subjects in each of three groups.

Case	MethodA Apt	MethodA Ach	Case	MethodB Apt	MethodB Ach	Case	MethodC Apt	MethodC Ach
1	32	62	7	21	72	13	38	95
2	46	66	8	24	85	14	45	88
3	27	64	9	18	61	15	52	104
4	35	48	10	32	87	16	48	86
5	31	51	11	35	69	17	41	72
6	40	74	12	26	74	18	37	63

Step by Step
1. Click **File**, **New**, and **Data**.
2. Click the **Variable View** tab at the bottom of your screen and when the Variable View screen appears define the Variables by typing **apt** (aptitude) in the first row, **ach** (achievement) in the second row and **group** in the third row.
3. Now go back to your **Data View** screen and enter the data as follows:

Case	Apt	Ach	Group
1	32	62	1
2	46	66	1
3	27	64	1
4	35	48	1
5	31	51	1
6	40	74	1
7	21	72	2

Continue on down to:

18	37	63	3

Save as **PROBU**.

4. Click **Analyze**, **General Linear Model**, and **Univariate**.

5. Click **Ach** and move to the **Dependent Variable box**.
6. Click **group** and move to **Fixed Factors box**.
7. Click **Apt** and move to **Covariate box**.
8. Click **OK**.

Selected Output

Univariate Analysis of Variance

Between-Subjects Factors

		N
group	1.00	6
	2.00	6
	3.00	6

Tests of Between-Subjects Effects

Source	Type III Sum of Squares	df	Mean Square	F	Sig.
Corrected Model	2206.515[a]	3	735.505	6.461	.006
Intercept	888.276	1	888.276	7.803	.014
apt	487.737	1	487.737	4.284	.057
group	1499.400	2	749.700	6.586	.010
Error	1593.763	14	113.840		
Total	100747.000	18			
Corrected Total	3800.278	17			

a. R Squared = .581 (Adjusted R Squared = .491)

We interpret this on the basis of the GROUP F ratio of 6.586, which is significant at .01. Therefore when the covariance analysis was used to equate the groups statistically, (which was necessary because the groups differed on aptitude at the beginning of training), the different teaching methods produced significantly different scores on the DV (the Math Achievement test).

Conclusions:

A one-way between subjects ANCOVA was computed to determine whether different teaching methods produced different math achievement scores with the math aptitude covariate being equated. Aptitude was not significantly related to Math Achievement, $(F(1,14) = 4.284, p > .05)$. However, the main effect for teaching method significantly influenced Math achievement $(F(2,14) = 6.586, p < .01)$.

PROBLEM V

Factorial ANCOVA

This procedure becomes appropriate when there are two or more IVs and at least one covariate. The next problem is based on whether scores on an actual flight exam are influenced by whether the subjects went to an approved ground school or studied at home on their own. Also, another IV was introduced, based on whether the subjects were allowed to watch a Flight School Video or not. In order to control for possible differences in pilot aptitude, an aptitude test was given to each trainee before any training took place. For this problem, the aptitude scores will be used as the covariate. The DV will be their measured performance in flying a plane, and the IVs will be whether they attended ground school and whether they used the training video. The data follow:

		No Video			Video	
	Case	Apt	Perf	Case	Apt	Perf
	1	62	5	11	46	5
	2	75	7	12	53	4
Ground School	3	41	3	13	57	3
	4	88	8	14	40	7
	5	72	7	15	62	6
	6	84	2	16	58	9
	7	91	3	17	72	10
No School	8	68	1	18	61	8
	9	77	1	19	65	8
	10	85	3	20	59	10

Now, for SPSS the scores have to be rearranged according to Groups. Call Ground School 1, and No Ground school 2. Also, call No Video 1 and Video 2.

Step by Step

1. Click **File**, **New**, and **Data**.
2. Click the **Variable View** tab at the bottom of your screen and when the Variable View screen appears define the Variables by typing **ap**t (aptitude) in the first row, **perf** (performance) in the second row, **school** in the third row and **video** in the fourth row.
3. Click back to the Data View screen and enter the scores as shown below.

Case	apt	perf	school	video
1	62	5	1	1
2	75	7	1	1
3	41	3	1	1
4	88	8	1	1
5	72	7	1	1
6	84	2	2	1
7	91	3	2	1
8	68	1	2	1
9	77	1	2	1
10	85	3	2	1
11	46	5	1	2
12	53	4	1	2

13	57	3	1	2
14	40	7	1	2
15	62	6	1	2
16	58	9	2	2
17	72	10	2	2
18	61	8	2	2
19	65	8	2	2
20	59	10	2	2

Save as **PROBV**.

4. Click **Analyze**.
5. Click **General Linear** and **Univariate**.
6. Enter **perf** (performance) as the **Dependent Variable**.
7. Enter both **school** and **video** as the Independent Variables (**Fixed Factors**).
8. Enter **apt** (Aptitude) as the covariate.
9. Click **OK**.

SELECTED OUTPUT

Tests of Between-Subjects Effects

Dependent Variable: perf

Source	Type III Sum of Squares	df	Mean Square	F	Sig.
Corrected Model	136.244[a]	4	34.061	22.452	.000
Intercept	.127	1	.127	.084	.776
apt	11.244	1	11.244	7.412	.016
school	3.151	1	3.151	2.077	.170
video	52.958	1	52.958	34.909	.000
school * video	82.837	1	82.837	54.605	.000
Error	22.756	15	1.517		
Total	764.000	20			
Corrected Total	159.000	19			

a. R Squared = .857 (Adjusted R Squared = .819)

We will be looking at three F ratios, Video, School and School*Video. All these F ratios assume that the groups have now been statistically equated on the basis of pilot aptitude. F for School = 2.077. Therefore there is no Performance difference regardless of whether they went to Ground School. F for Video = 34.909. This F ratio is clearly significant and indicates that watching the Video had a strong effect. F for School*Video = 54.605. Again, this F ratio is significant, and the best way to interpret this is via the graph. Find the means for each condition

	No Video	Video
No Ground School	Cell A (m = 6.000)	Cell B (m = 5.000)
Ground School	Cell C (m = 2.000)	Cell C (m = 9.000)

54

Graph the results by placing the columns (Video vs. no Video) under the abscissa and Ground vs. no Ground school on the y ordinate. If the graph lines cross, there is visual evidence of an interaction. From where we left off above, continue now with

Step-by-Step (the graph)
10. Instead of OK, back at step 10, click **plots** and move video into the **horizontal box** and school into the **separate lines box**.
11. Click **Add, Continue**, and **OK**.

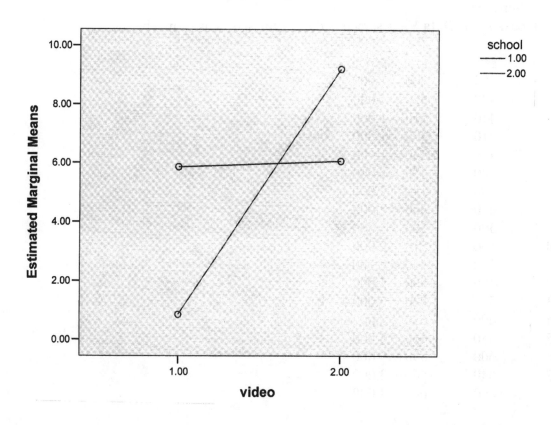

Estimated Marginal Means of perf

Conclusions:
A factorial ANCOVA was computed to determine if the two variables, Ground School versus no Ground School and Video versus no Video produced a difference in pilot performance, with the aptitude variable being covaried out. Whether the person went to Ground School did not significantly affect pilot performance ($F(1,15) = 2.077$, $p<.05$). Whether the video was shown, however, did impact pilot performance ($F(1,15) = 34.909$, $p<.01$). Also, there was a significant interaction ($F(1,15) = 54.605$, $p<.01$). The Video was most effective for those students who had attended Ground School.

PROBLEM W

MANOVA
MANOVA provides a multivariate analysis and is therefore used whenever we have more than ONE DEPENDENT variable. Assume that we wish to discover whether SAT and GRE scores are a function of past schooling. We select 6 subjects from each of 3 types of schools (Groups), public schools, parochial schools and private schools. The groups (schools) will be labeled 1. for public, 2. for parochial and 3. for private.

Step by Step
1. Click **File, New,** and **Data.**
2. Click the **Variable View** tab at the bottom of your screen and when the Variable View screen appears define the Variables by typing **sat** in the first row, **gre** in the second row, and **group** in the third row.
3. Click back to the **Data View** screen and enter the scores as shown below.

Case	sat	gre	group
1	480	500	1.000
2	420	520	1.000
3	450	510	1.000
4	410	400	1.000
5	480	530	1.000
6	480	480	1.000
7	500	590	2.000
8	640	650	2.000
9	500	500	2.000
10	500	510	2.000
11	580	590	2.000
12	490	500	2.000
13	520	520	3.000
14	690	630	3.000
15	650	660	3.000
16	600	590	3.000
17	640	560	3.000
18	600	600	3.000

   Save as **PROBW.**
4. Click **Analyze.**
5. Click **General Linear Model** and **Multivariate.**
6. Put both **sat** and **gre** in the **Dependent Variable box.**
7. Put **Group** in the Independent Variable (**FIXED FACTORS**) box.
8. Click **OK**

Now comes the hard part. You have to sort out from all that output what you need for a basic interpretation.

Selected Output
Skip by intercept and Pillai's Trace and go Down to GROUP.

Multivariate Tests[c]

Effect		Value	F	Hypothesis df	Error df	Sig.
Intercept	Pillai's Trace	.993	1005.627[a]	2.000	14.000	.000
	Wilks' Lambda	.007	1005.627[a]	2.000	14.000	.000
	Hotelling's Trace	143.661	1005.627[a]	2.000	14.000	.000
	Roy's Largest Root	143.661	1005.627[a]	2.000	14.000	.000
group	Pillai's Trace	.715	4.171	4.000	30.000	.008
	Wilks' Lambda	.315	5.481[a]	4.000	28.000	.002
	Hotelling's Trace	2.086	6.780	4.000	26.000	.001
	Roy's Largest Root	2.041	15.304[b]	2.000	15.000	.000

a. Exact statistic

b. The statistic is an upper bound of F that yields a lower bound on the significance level.

c. Design: Intercept+group

Wilks' Lambda is a test of mean differences, but as an inverse measure it is interpreted unlike those statistics we have been covering. That is, with Wilks' Lambda the **smaller** the value the more likely it will lead to a **reject** of Null. Since the overall Lambda for group is clearly significant at .002, we can now examine the between-subjects effects.

Again, skip down past Corrected Model and intercept and go to group.

Source	Dependent Variable	Type III Sum of Squares	df	Mean Square	F	Sig.
Corrected Model	sat	80033.333[a]	2	40016.667	14.706	.000
	gre	32933.333[b]	2	16466.667	5.735	.014
Intercept	sat	5152050.000	1	5152050.000	1893.363	.000
	gre	5379200.000	1	5379200.000	1873.560	.000
group	sat	80033.333	2	40016.667	14.706	.000
	gre	32933.333	2	16466.667	5.735	.014
Error	sat	40816.667	15	2721.111		
	gre	43066.667	15	2871.111		
Total	sat	5272900.000	18			
	gre	5455200.00	18			
Corrected Total	sat	120850.000	17			
	gre	76000.000	17			

a. R Squared = .662 (Adjusted R Squared = .617

b. R Squared = .433 (Adjusted R Squared = .358

Conclusion:
A one-way MANOVA was computed looking at the effects of past schooling (public, parochial, private) on SAT and GRE scores. A significant effect was found (Lambda = .315 and F (4,28) = 5.481, p < .01). Follow-up univariate ANOVAS found significant differences for SAT (F(2,15) = 14.706, p < .01), and for GRE (F(2,15) = 5.735, p < .01). GRE scores were significantly higher than SAT scores for both public and parochial schools. Private schools were significantly higher than parochial or public schools on both SAT and GRE, and parochial schools were higher than public schools on both SAT and GRE.

Now, if Lambda had been, say, .828 with an F ratio of .693, then we would conclude that a one-way MANOVA was computed looking at the effects of past schooling (public, parochial, private) on SAT and GRE scores. No significant effect was found (Lambda = .828. F(4,18) = .693, p > .05). Neither SAT nor GRE was influenced by past schooling.

PROBLEM X

Discriminant Analysis
This procedure is best thought of as a reverse ANOVA or MANOVA. In an ANOVA the researcher takes two or more groups and then compares their scores on the dependent variable in order to see if the scores on the dependent variable were influenced by the action of the independent variable. With discriminant analysis, however, we take the scores on the dependent variable and use them in order to predict the group membership, which is typically the independent variable (just the opposite of the ANOVA). That is, we will use the DV scores to classify the subjects into groups. This is an extremely valuable technique, especially when the researcher is involved in data mining (using already existing data pools). Using the data shown below, we will attempt to classify our subjects (in this case inmates) with regard to whether they had or had not been previously incarcerated. Thus, we will attempt to discover if scores on an alcohol abuse test, a drug abuse test and an anger test significantly predict group membership.

Step by Step
1. Click **File**, **New**, and **Data**.
2. Click the **Variable View** tab at the bottom of your screen and when the Variable View screen appears define the Variables by typing **alcohol** in the first row, **drug** in the second row, **anger** in the third row and **group** in the fourth row.
3. Click back to the **Data View** screen and enter the scores as shown below. For the group variable, use 1 to indicate the inmate has never been incarcerated before and 2 to indicate a previous incarceration.

Case	alcohol	drug	anger	group
1	14	12	290	2
2	6	10	240	1
3	5	8	180	1
4	12	10	210	1
5	8	7	185	1
6	15	12	230	1
7	10	8	225	2

Scores continue.

8	8	10	260	1
9	11	8	290	2
10	9	10	230	2
11	14	12	290	2
12	6	10	240	1
13	5	8	180	1
14	12	10	210	1
15	8	7	185	1
16	15	12	230	2
17	10	8	225	2
18	8	10	260	2
19	11	8	290	2
20	9	10	230	2

Save as **PROBX**.

4. Click **Analyze**, **Classify** and **Discriminant**.
5. Click **group** and move it to the **Grouping Variable box**.
6. Click **Define Range** and enter **1** for **minimum** and **2** for **maximum**.
7. Click **Continue**.
8. Click **alcohol**, **drug** and **anger** and move them to the **Independents box**.
9. Click **Statistics** and click **means** and **univariate ANOVAS**.
10. Click all four options in the **Matrices box**.
11. Click **Continue** and **Classify**.
12. Click **All Groups Equal** – use this option even if the two sample groups are of unequal size but represent equal proportions of the population. Otherwise click Compute from Group Sizes.
13. Click **Combined Groups** in the **Plot Box** and **Within Groups** in the **Covariance Matrix box**.
14. Click **Summary Table** in the **Display box** and **Continue**.
15. IMPORTANT – Click **Save** and **Predicted Group Membership**.
16. Click **Continue** and **OK**.

SELECTED OUTPUT

Group Statistics

group		Mean	Std. Deviation	Valid N (listwise)	
				Unweighted	Weighted
1.00	alcohol	8.5000	3.40751	10	10.000
	drug	9.2000	1.61933	10	10.000
	anger	212.0000	29.26887	10	10.000
2.00	alcohol	11.1000	2.42441	10	10.000
	drug	9.8000	1.75119	10	10.000
	anger	256.0000	30.89408	10	10.000
Total	alcohol	9.8000	3.17225	20	20.000
	drug	9.5000	1.67017	20	20.000
	anger	234.0000	36.97795	20	20.000

Here we see the means and standard deviations for each group, separately as well as for both groups combined. Notice that all three means are higher in the 2 group (previously incarcerated) than in the 1 group (no previous incarcerations).

As said above, Discriminant Analysis is a back-fit technique, and consistent with this counter-intuitive model, the significance level is based on the Wilks' Lambda. This is a multivariate test of GROUP differences over the selected variables. It is calculated on the basis of Eigen values, and because it is an inverse measure it is interpreted such that the smaller the value of Lambda the more likely it will lead to a reject of Null. That is, the lower the Lambda value (those near zero) the higher the level of discrimination power. Also note that the accompanying chi square can be used to test the Lambda for significance.

Now skip down to Wilks' Lambda and note the overall significance level of .021.

Wilks' Lambda

Test of Function(s)	Wilks' Lambda	Chi-square	df	Sig.
1	.555	9.708	3	.021

And now the last table we need: the Classification Results.

			Predicted Group Membership		
		group	1.00	2.00	Total
Original	Count	1.00	8	2	10
		2.00	2	8	10
	%	1.00	80.0	20.0	100.0
		2.00	20.0	80.0	100.0

a. 80.0% of original grouped cases correctly classified.

And take special note of that last line, the line we've all been waiting for
a. **80.0% of original grouped cases correctly classified,** which tells us that the when using those variables (alcohol, drug and anger), the probability of predicting the correct group, that is the recidivists versus the non-recidivists, is .800. Not too bad.

Now go back to your file of scores and print it out. It will tell you exactly which cases were misclassified. The misclassified subjects in the above example were numbers 6, 8, 10, and 20.

Conclusions:
A discriminant analysis was conducted to find out whether three variables, alcohol score, drug score and anger score, could be used to predict whether an inmate had been previously incarcerated. The Wilks' Lambda was significant (Lambda = .555), at .021, meaning that the discriminant function produced a significant difference between the two target groups. The predictors correctly classified the inmates with an accuracy of 80.0%.

PROBLEM Y

Mixed ANOVA Split Plot

This is the analysis to use if one of the IVs is between subjects and another IV is within subjects. Take the following example. A researcher was interested in providing the best instructional video for teaching college students how to use an SPSS statistical program. There were three separate videos provided. After the video was shown all students were then tested in Trial 1. Then after an hour of practice they were tested in Trial 2, and finally after another hour of practice, they were tested for the last time in Trial 3. Thus, this problem has two IVs. One IV is a within subjects (in this case "trials", from trial 1 to trial 2 to trial 3, and the other IV is between subjects, in this case which of three Video Instruction Sets the students were exposed to.

Step by Step

1. Click **File**, **New**, and **Data**.
2. Click the **Variable View** tab at the bottom of your screen and when the Variable View screen appears define the Variables by typing **trial1** in the first row, **trial 2** in the second row, **trial 3** in the third row and **group** in the fourth row. Click back to the **Data View** screen and enter the scores as shown below.

Case	trial1	trial2	trial3	group
1	54	62	67	1
2	77	89	87	1
3	66	75	79	1
4	57	67	69	1
5	62	75	73	1
6	72	86	84	1
7	71	83	84	1
8	45	62	67	2
9	76	96	98	2
10	59	75	83	2
11	66	84	91	2
12	62	75	85	2
13	51	65	74	2
14	69	83	93	2
15	59	77	95	3
16	55	75	87	3
17	47	63	81	3
18	69	91	98	3
19	59	81	92	3
20	56	73	90	3
21	56	72	90	3

Save as **PROBY**.

3. Click **Analyze**.
4. Click **General Linear Model**.
5. Click **Repeated Measures**, and type the **Within Factor** as **trials** with **3** levels.

6. Click **Add** and **Define**.
7. Then on this new screen (Repeated Measures) put **trial1**, **trial2** and **trial3** in the **Within Subjects box** and **group** in the **Between Subjects box**.
8. Click **Options** and select **Descriptives**.
9. Click **Continue** and **OK**.

Selected Output

Relax, you won't need all that output for a very basic analysis.

First, examine the descriptives and notice that you have means and standard deviations for each of the groups for each of the trials.

Descriptive Statistics

	group	Mean	Std. Deviation	N
trial2	1.00	76.7143	9.94509	7
	2.00	77.1429	11.71080	7
	3.00	76.0000	8.62168	7
	Total	76.6190	9.66166	21
trial3	1.00	77.5714	7.95523	7
	2.00	84.4286	10.92180	7
	3.00	90.4286	5.50325	7
	Total	84.1429	9.63476	21
trial1	1.00	65.5714	8.38366	7
	2.00	61.1429	10.60548	7
	3.00	57.2857	6.55017	7
	Total	61.3333	8.92935	21

Next, look at the Multivariate tests, and focus on the Wilks' Lambda, which gives an .002 for trials and a .016 for trials by group. Both are significant at <.01. The differences are significant.

Multivariate Tests[c]

Effect		Value	F	Hypothesis df	Error df	Sig.
trials	Pillai's Trace	.998	4518.779[a]	2.000	17.000	.000
	Wilks' Lambda	.002	4518.779[a]	2.000	17.000	.000
	Hotelling's Trace	531.621	4518.779[a]	2.000	17.000	.000
	Roy's Largest Root	531.621	4518.779[a]	2.000	17.000	.000
trials * group	Pillai's Trace	1.006	9.101	4.000	36.000	.000
	Wilks' Lambda	.016	58.996[a]	4.000	34.000	.000
	Hotelling's Trace	60.703	242.811	4.000	32.000	.000
	Roy's Largest Root	60.681	546.125[b]	2.000	18.000	.000

Now glance at the Mauchly Test, which computes to .307 and is significant at < .01.

This means that we cannot assume sphericity, so rather than reading the significance Level for Sphericity Assumed, we will use the Greenhouse–Geisser value. When the Mauchly is rejected, the df are usually adjusted to make the analysis more conservative. In this particular case the values are identical, both provide F ratios of 817.954 – BUT THAT'S NOT ALWAYS THE CASE. A word to the wise—always check your Mauchlys.

Mauchly's Test of Sphericity[b]

Measure: MEASURE_1

Within Subjects Effect	Mauchly's W	Approx. Chi-Square	df	Sig.
trials	.307	20.071	2	.000

Tests the null hypothesis that the error covariance matrix of the orthonormalized transformed dependent variable is proportional to an identity matrix.

Next, go down to the Tests of Within Subject Effects.

Tests of Within-Subjects Effects

Measure: MEASURE_1

Source		Type III Sum of Squares	df	Mean Square	F	Sig.
trials	Sphericity Assumed	5673.746	2	2836.873	817.954	.000
	Greenhouse-Geisser	5673.746	1.181	4802.586	817.954	.000
	Huynh-Feldt	5673.746	1.356	4183.583	817.954	.000
	Lower-bound	5673.746	1.000	5673.746	817.954	.000
trials * group	Sphericity Assumed	806.063	4	201.516	58.103	.000
	Greenhouse-Geisser	806.063	2.363	341.149	58.103	.000
	Huynh-Feldt	806.063	2.712	297.179	58.103	.000
	Lower-bound	806.063	2.000	403.032	58.103	.000
Error (trials)	Sphericity Assumed	124.857	36	3.468		
	Greenhouse-Geisser	124.857	21.265	5.871		
	Huynh-Feldt	124.857	24.411	5.115		
	Lower-bound	124.857	18.000	6.937		

Here we see the F ratios, with and without the sphericity assumption. The F for trials is 817.954 and is significant at <.01, and the F for trials by group is 58.103 – also significant at <.01.

The most important F ratios to look at are (1) the F ratio for within-effects for trials, which was 817.954, (2) the F ratio for the trial-by-group interaction, which was 58.103 and, finally, the F ratio for the between-subjects, which was .039. Also, examine the means to get a picture of the direction of the differences.

Tests of Between-Subjects Effects

Measure: MEASURE_1
Transformed Variable: Average

Source	Type III Sum of Squares	df	Mean Square	F	Sig.
Intercept	345284.063	1	345284.063	1422.688	.000
group	18.698	2	9.349	.039	.962
Error	4368.571	18	242.698		

Conclusions:

A 3 X 3 mixed design was calculated to examine the effects of the instructional video (groups 1, 2 and 3) and trials (trial1, trial2 and trial3) on test scores. A significant trial x group interaction was present, $F(4,36) = 58.103$, $p < .001$. In addition, the main effect for trials was significant $F(2,36)=817.954$, $p < .001$. Note that the means increased as the trials increased, (m=61.333 for trial 1, m=76.619 for trial 2 and m=84.143 for trial 3). The main effect for group (type of video) was not significant $F(2,18) = .039$, $p > .05$. The means for the groups were virtually the same (m=73.286 for group 1, m=74.238 for group 2, and m=74.571 for group 3. Examination of the data indicates that Video Group 3 showed the most improvement in scores over trials.

Now for a "what if"? Suppose the F ratios had not been significant. We will now use different F values to show how to explain a lack of significance. If the F RATIOS HAD NOT BEEN SIGNIFICANT, we would conclude that a 3 X 3 mixed design was calculated to examine the effects of the video (1, 2 and 3) and trials (trial 1, trial 2 and trial 3) on test scores. No significant main effects or interactions were found. The trial x group interaction $F(4,36) = 1.10$, $p > .05$, the main effect for trial $F(2,36)=1.95$, $p > .05$, and the main effect for group $F(2,18) = .039$, $p > .05$ were all found to be non-significant. Thus, the test scores were not influenced by either trials or video group or any combination of the two.

PROBLEM Z

Factor Analysis

Factor analysis is based on an attempt to reduce the number of variables by looking for clusters of highly correlated variables that are independent of other clusters. Those highly correlated clusters are called factors, and are assumed to be measuring the same underlying trait. For this problem, we will use an **extremely shortened** data set, but again it's better to spend your time analyzing the factors than typing in hundreds of scores on dozens of variables. The following limited data will be based on a school program that started in Arkansas and has now spread to many other states. The schools are now measuring a child's body mass, called a body mass index (BMI) and then the results are sent home (like a report card). Imagine how you'd feel if you or your child flunked Body Mass.

We will be using four variables for this study: 1. The Mother's weight, which may relate to a child's BMI through either DNA or household diet, or both). 2. The child's IQ. 3. The child's scores on a spelling test and 4. The child's BMI.

Step by Step

1. Click **File**, **New**, and **Data**.
2. Click the **Variable View** tab at the bottom of your screen and when the Variable View screen appears define the Variables by typing **mother** in the first row, **iq** in the second row, **spell** in the third row, and **bmi** in the fourth row.
3. Click back to the **Data View** screen and enter the scores as shown below.

Case	mother	iq	spell	bmi
1	120	110	12	55
2	110	120	18	25
3	122	115	15	60
4	125	115	15	75
5	140	118	16	85
6	121	112	10	50
7	112	116	16	40
8	115	114	16	50
9	135	113	15	80
10	100	117	17	20

Once the data are in be sure to file save, in this case call it **PROBZ**.

4. Click **Analyze**.
5. Click **Data Reduction** and **Factor**.
6. Put all four variables **mother, iq, spell** and **bmi** in the **Variables box**.
7. Check **Descriptives,** and then **Univariate descriptives**.
8. Check **Initial solution** and **Reproduced**.
9. Click **Continue** and **Extraction**.
10. Check **Correlation matrix, Unrotated factor solution** and **Scree Plot**.
11. Check **Eigenvalues over 1**.
12. Click **Continue, Rotation, Varimax** and **Rotated Solution**.
13. Click **Continue** and **Scores**.
14. Check **Save as Variables** and **Regression**.
15. Click **Continue** and **Options**.
16. Check **Sorted by Size, Continue** and **OK**

SPSS will then select the cluster of variables whose shared correlations explain the most variance. Then a second factor (the next grouping) is extracted that explains the most variability AFTER the first factor has been culled. That is, SPSS pulls out the factor that explains the second-most variability. This process continues for a third, fourth etc. For each factor there will be an eigenvalue. The first factor always has the highest eigenvalue. It then lists the % of variance accounted for by that eigenvalue, followed by a cumulative **percent**. For each successive factor, the eigenvalues will get smaller and continue on down until they reach 1.00. Now which factors should you concentrate on? Keep those factors that seem to have some construct or theoretical validity. To do this begin by selecting on the basis of a quantitative criterion, the default is an eigenvalue larger than 1.00 (less than 1.00 explains less variance than a single variable). Once the factors are selected they should be rotated in order to get high factor loadings on one factor and low loads on all others. SPSS uses VARIMAX rotation (orthogonal) because the axes are rotated in such a way as to remain at right angles to each other (which keeps them independent). For a larger data set, go to SPSS.com and select schools.sav. For more on this and a more complete discussion of Factor Analysis see (Mertler and Vannatta, 2001).

Selected Output
This first screen will give you the means and standard deviations for each of the variables, that is for mother's weight, child's IQ, child's spelling scores and the child's BMI.

Factor Analysis

Descriptive Statistics

	Mean	Std. Deviation	Analysis N
mother	120.0000	11.75679	10
iq	115.0000	2.94392	10
spell	15.0000	2.35702	10
bmi	54.0000	21.95956	10

Next, look at the correlation matrix (labeled as Reproduced Correlations), which will give you the actual Pearson r values for each bivariate combination. Even here you can begin to see which variables are clustering. Notice the significant correlation between mother's weight and child's BMI. Also note the significant correlation between the child's IQ and spelling score.

Reproduced Correlations

		mother	iq	spell	bmi
Reproduced Correlation	mother	.980[b]	-.234	-.250	.978
	iq	-.234	.918[b]	.916	-.277
	spell	-.250	.916	.915[b]	-.293
	bmi	.978	-.277	-.293	.979[b]
Residual[a]	mother		.022	-.023	-.021
	iq	.022		-.084	-.024
	spell	-.023	-.084		.025
	bmi	-.021	-.024	.025	

Extraction Method: Principal Component Analysis.
  a. Residuals are computed between observed and reproduced correlations. There are 1 (16.0%) nonredundant residuals with absolute values greater than 0.05.
  b. Reproduced communalities

Examine the Total Variance Explained table, which gives the Eigen values for each factor. Those with Eigen values greater than 1 should be retained (that is for component-factors 1 and 2).

Total Variance Explained

Component	Initial Eigenvalues		
	Total	% of Variance	Cumulative %
1	2.426	60.650	60.650
2	1.365	34.136	94.787
3	.183	4.563	99.349
4	.026	.651	100.000

Extraction Method: Principal Component Analysis.

Next, look over the Scree Plot. One should keep all components (factors) within the sharp descent, before the Eigen values level off (Mertler and Vannatta, 2001).

Scree Plot

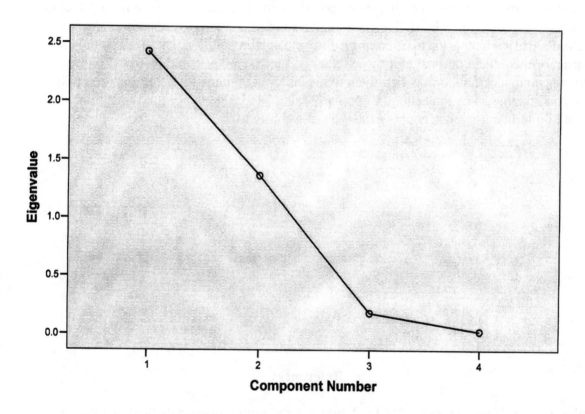

Rotated Component Matrix

Finally, examining this matrix makes it clear that we have two independent components, with Component 1 (mother's weight and BMI) at .983 and .976, and Component 2 (IQ and spelling scores) at .950 and .946.

Rotated Component Matrix[a]

	Component	
	1	2
mother	.983	-.116
bmi	.976	-.163
iq	-.126	.950
spell	-.143	.946

Extraction Method: Principal Component Analysis.
Rotation Method: Varimax with Kaiser Normalization.

a. Rotation converged in 3 interations.

Conclusions:

A factor analysis was performed on a four-variable input, mother's weight, child's IQ, child's spelling scores, and child's BMI. Two factors were sorted. Factor 1 combined mother's weight and child's BMI, whereas Factor 2 combined IQ and spelling ability. There is certainly a construct or theoretical rationale for these factors. The first factor could be based on an hereditary predisposition, or the diet given to the children at home (or a combination of both). The second factor can be understood as perhaps being based on overall intelligence and that portion of intelligence that accounts for the child's ability to spell.

References

Mertler, C.A. & Vannatta, R.A. (2001). Advanced and multivariate statistical methods. Los Angeles, CA: Pyrczak Publishing.

Sprinthall, R.C. (2007). Basic statistical analysis. Boston, MA: Allyn and Bacon.

INDEX

Fixed factors, 23, 52, 54, 57
Friedman ANOVA, 43, 45

G
General factors, 54
General linear model, 52, 56, 62
Goodness of fit, 26
Graphs, 2, 16
Greenhouse–Geisser test, 37, 63
Grouping variable, 14, 41, 59

H
H test (Kruskal–Wallis), 40
Histogram, 9
Holden Psychological Screening Inventory
        (HPSI), 15, 16
Homogeneity of variance, 15, 20, 21, 22
Hypothesis, 12, 13, 33, 35, 37, 38, 40, 42, 43

I
Independent t, 15, 38
Independent variable (IV), 16, 19, 22, 23, 25,
        29, 30, 32, 35, 53, 54, 57, 58, 61
Initial solution, 65
Inserting, 4
Interaction, 22, 24, 25, 56, 64
Internal consistency, 45, 49
Interval data, 3, 17, 43, 46
IQ scores, 2, 4, 8, 9, 11, 32, 33, 44, 45, 51, 65,
        66, 68
Item analysis, 45, 48

K
Keep estimates, 30
Kurtosis, 8, 9

L
Lambda (Wilks), 57, 58, 60, 62
Levene's test, 15, 21, 22
LSI, 15, 16, 44, 45

M
Main effects, 22, 24, 25
Mann–Whitney U test, 38, 39
MANOVA, 56, 58
Matched samples, 42, 43
Mauchly test of sphericity, 37, 63
Maximum value, 8
Mean, 9, 11–14, 20, 21, 23, 32, 33, 35, 36, 38,
        39, 55, 57, 59, 60, 62–64, 66
Median, 8, 9